AF491380

# LIES & CIGARS, MAGAZINES & POCKETBOOKS

# Lies & Cigars, Magazines & Pocketbooks

## *A Little Bit of Everything*

KODY CHRISTIANSEN

Heartbreak Dreams Publishing

Instagram/X: @kodykitty
Facebook: /kodychristiansen
LinkedIn: /in/kodychristiansen/

Copyright © 2024 by Kody Christiansen

All rights reserved. No part of this book may be repro-
duced in any manner whatsoever without written permis-
sion except in the case of brief quotations embodied in
critical articles and reviews. All photos are from the
author's personal collection.

First Edition
First Printing, 2024

# Contents

# MAGAZINES



# POCKETBOOKS

# Dedication

*David, my Giles, you left us too soon.*

*Annette, my German sister, and dear friend,*

*wish you were still here.*

To all those I consider *my water* - my chosen family all over the world - thank you for your love and support.

And to all those unafraid to take a chance on yourselves - this one is for you.

# Foreword

The journey Kody Christiansen has taken in his life is both confounding and exhilarating to those of us who have witnessed it up close and personal. In his first two autobiographical books, I was always amazed that he so fearlessly exposed his strengths and frailties. I've met people who only knew him as a drug and alcohol-addicted lost cause, who always asked if he was still alive. While others have only known the driven academic and activist whose ambition knows no bounds.

Kody's story is truly a Dr. Jekyll and Mr. Hyde tale. His life is both transparent and opaque. This third installment of his memoirs raises the curtain on both the events that shaped him into the person he is today as well as the menacing forces that wanted to keep him down. It also exhibits the artistic talents that lay dormant during his troubled years.

He often calls me his surrogate father. It's a role that has brought me both profound sadness as well as compelling pride. Ten years ago, I was picking him up off the floor in a drunken stupor. Last year, I watched him graduate from Harvard University. But even in the darkest times, I knew a gem existed under that hardened exterior he had built around himself. In this new memoir, he exposes his literary, academic, and artistic talents. It's a tribute to him as well as a personal triumph for me as the paternal figure helping him bloom and prosper.

Thomas Rosa
Cake and Art
West Hollywood, CA

# Prologue

*Lies & Cigars, Magazines & Pocketbooks* is a compilation of untold true tales, poignant poetry, artistic endeavors, and academic papers that are intimately presented in a book that was inspired by a sign above a defunct convenience store in Astoria, Queens.

A few years ago, on one of my cat-sitting adventures for my dear friend (more like a mom, really), Aimee, I came across this sign and took a black and white photo. The photo stayed in my phone all this time - but it was also burned into my memory. It called to me to tell some of the stories from my life not featured in my other memoirs - stories from before the *Hollywood Heartbreak* that led to *New York Dreams* and after the *One Week in LA*, where unbelievable magic and divine intervention led to world headline news. The sign, with its strange mix of items, motivated me to share a collection of my own strange and beautiful works that probably never would have seen the light of day if it weren't for this book.

I searched my cloud high and low, dusted off old CD ROMs, and rummaged through Facebook memories to find hidden treasures that, when put all together, make up an emotional hodgepodge of adventures, pain, love, and life. These stories want to be told. So, here they are. Completely incomplete.

So, why do I write books? (A question I get quite often.) There are two personal answers to this question, really. *One*: it is always cathartic to put down into words some stories that might be difficult to retell. Sometimes, releasing them from the lockbox of our memories frees space in our minds and souls for something new, something better, to take its place. It lifts an invisible but palpable weight from our emotional core. *Two*: Connection. I feel so unbelievably blessed to still get emails or direct messages from people who have read my books telling me how they have been helped or inspired in some way. They quit drinking, they followed dreams they thought they could no longer achieve, they reconnected with people, or they just learned to love themselves once again. *This is definitely the most important of the two reasons.*

When the words are released, and connections are made with people who see their story in my own - that's how I know I have done something meaningful and impactful. If one person is changed or discovers something new about themselves or takes another path that leads them to a better space because they read my words - then I have done my job.

Life is a continuous cycle of education. "Learn

something new every day," *THEY* say. I have tried to live by those words since the day I found my lasting sobriety. Reading books, watching television shows, listening to friends, falling deeply into songs, and taking classes on subjects I never thought I would explore - have all helped me continue to grow. So, I hope you take a little something from the words and pictures in this book, maybe learn something new ... about another side of life... or learn a little bit more about yourself.

No matter what, I hope you find something within these pages to connect to, and, in the end, I hope you never forget to Stay Strong and Dream Big. All things are truly possible when you take a chance on yourself.

Here we go...

# LIES

Unfinished Stories

# Lies

"I'll be there at noon to pick you up."
"This weekend it will be just you and me."
"I'll have some time this summer."
"Something came up, son."

Something always came up. There was always some excuse to leave a little boy sitting on the back of the couch with tears in his eyes glued to the quiet street right outside his windows.

"My #1 son," he always called me. But I never felt like number one in his life.

It's funny how we can sometimes look back at the exact moments or relationships that shaped our behaviors or pet peeves as adults. How we can pinpoint when our innocence is chipped away - oftentimes by the ones we love the most.

It was my absent father that did it to me. Made me untrusting of men — and made me detest tardiness.

It's like, even though I am an adult, every time someone is late to a date or even just a friendly meet-up, that hurt little boy in the back of my mind starts worrying, wondering, and whining. "They aren't coming. He isn't coming. You aren't worth it," the voice whispers so quietly it's mostly inaudible. But it's there. It's always there. No matter how old we get, how many Ivy League colleges we attend, or jobs that have come and gone, or families made and lost - the most impactful little traumas lay dormant just waiting for their chance to crawl their way out from the darkness.

I don't have an easy answer for how to deal with it. I DO know that alcohol and drugs are NEVER the answer, though. I went through so much unnecessary hell because I used those things to quiet that voice that screamed, "You are not enough."

There were too many times when I believed that voice. (Not having my mother around to lift me up as I went from high school senior to orphaned adult which only added to the volume of it.) There was just so much pain and an incredible sense of regret that no 18-year-old should ever have to feel. But that was my life.

This is my life.
A little bit of everything.

# Chapter 1

# The Book That Almost Was

Holiday in my Hometown

# Holiday in my Hometown

## *Prologue*

Just months had passed since the story in "One Week in LA," and I was about to take another trip that was long overdue. After successfully facing my fears and conquering them in Hollywood, I decided I would continue on the brave path and return to somewhere even more important. My hometown.

With the glowing reception of acceptance I received in Los Angeles still fresh in my mind, I figured it was the perfect time to head back to Fort Worth, Texas. It had been many years since I had stepped foot onto the downtown asphalt that I had left so quickly to pursue my dreams. I made up so many reasons in my mind over the years for why it was "never the right time to go back." But now, with my book out and winning awards, I felt like I could return with my head held high.

The first time I left the second-biggest state in the nation was a year after my mother passed away and just two semesters into my college studies at TCU. The weekend my college choir performed at Carnegie Hall, I was asked by a gay nightlife promoter to host my own "drag show" in New York City at one of the most popular "club kid" venues called Kurfew. That offer became the catalyst for some of my life's biggest adventures. But just a year and a half later, when the money from my structured settlement sale ran out, I made my way back to Texas. It would be a few more years before I ventured out again.

The second and final time I left Fort Worth, I was asked to audition for a role in the film "Miss Congeniality 2" in Hollywood, California. I booked the part; playing a Britney Spears drag queen! *So, basically, I was playing myself.* Haha. The week and a half I spent in LA got me hooked on the glitz and glamor of it all. It also didn't hurt that I had a week-long whirlwind romance with a gorgeous gay porn star who, by the end of my trip, told me he loved me and convinced me I had to come back, move in with him, and be his boyfriend. So, I did.

And that relationship lasted about as long as one of his videos...

But my relationship with Los Angeles had just begun, and it would be many years before I would leave the few-mile stretch that was the city of West Hollywood. It's not that I didn't want to travel or go see my Grandmother in Texas, but I had become so lost in the "glitz and glamor" that I started to forget who I was. And in this instance, when I say "glitz and glamor," I mean "drugs and alcohol."

After shuffling through different hostels and a job at a funky clothing store on Melrose, I finally found a great job managing a celebrity cake shop. The owner became like a father figure to me, and we used to fight like family, too. He cared deeply about me and was very disappointed when I would show up to work drunk or not come in at all. He really should have fired me many times over, but he always saw the good in me. He knew that if I could turn my life around, I could do big things. He was right. But it took time for me to figure it all out.

"Figuring it out" came after all the drama and enlightenment resulting from the journey chronicled in my first book, "Hollywood Heartbreak | New York Dreams." The spur-of-the-moment decision to leave everything behind in Hollywood, escape suicide and heartbreak, and get a fresh start in New York City. Homeless shelters served as the backdrop for my first year and a half in the city, but when I finally found my divine path (and sobriety), the world opened up to me, and my dreams started to come true. But during that first year in the shelters, I found out my Grandmother passed away, and that was the first time I really considered making my way back to Texas.

While I was in Hollywood, I kept up with my family and friends in Texas, but I always felt guilty about not going back to see my Grandma Ellen. I made empty promises to her all the time, saying, "I'll try to make it home when I can to see you," but I never did. Part of it was my addictions, and part of it was my ego. I couldn't bear to return to my hometown until I was something similar to the success, or the "star," I set out to be all those years ago when I left. I couldn't quite return to Hurst, Texas as a worthless, homeless, broken alcoholic. But after the shelters... my ego was gone. I was transformed into a more open-minded soul. A better version of myself that was now grateful for every little thing: physical, spiritual, and emotional.

So, I wrote my first book. "Hollywood Heartbreak | New York Dreams" won multiple book awards and received some pretty amazing press when one of the biggest stars in the world was caught by paparazzi carrying a copy in his hands. But none of that really mattered. What mattered was the letters I got from people telling me how the words in my book helped them to quit drinking or find the courage to follow some lost dream they thought impossible to achieve. That's what truly touched my heart and the reason I wrote the books in the first place.

I wish my Grandma would have been able to live long enough to see my books and the successes I am having now. But I know, like my mother, she is watching over me, and she is proud. So, in their memory, I decided to gather all my bravery and make another life-changing trip before the year ended. A trip back to my hometown where I hadn't stepped foot in a decade.

"You have to go back to where you came from to really appreciate where you are now." A personal quote from my big Hollywood book signing and one I had to truly put to the test now. Was I ready for what I might stumble upon while trekking through my past? I wasn't sure... but the plane tickets were already purchased and the book signing was set for three days before Christmas. Looks like I'd be spending the holiday in my hometown, once again. Many years later.

## Chapter 1 - These Boots Were Made for Walking (Down Memory Lane).

The plane touched down in Dallas, Texas, a little before noon. As I started to unbuckle my seat belt on the Virgin America 747, my mind started to race. It was just like when I landed in LA for the first time again after all the drama, homelessness, and sobriety, but this time, in Texas, there was an even stronger nervous energy surrounding me. It had been over a decade since I had been there, and I wondered if the places of my childhood had changed as much as I had, or would some things still be the same?

I exited the plane to follow the crowd to the luggage retrieval area but got lost momentarily in the surroundings. To my left, just outside the gate door, was a Texas boot shop! A big neon light shaped to look like the state was hung above the black awning. The medium-sized airport shop was filled from floor to ceiling with cowboy boots, leather belts, cowboy hats, ropes, and even spurs! It was a surefire sign that I was home. My original home.

I looked around for a moment, took a breath in deeply, and just soaked in the lingering scents of leather, hay, and snakeskin. It was an oddly comforting smell to me. One I hadn't even thought about in over a decade. It's funny how something so minuscule can make such big memories appear. Sense memories.

I walked around the shop for a minute, gliding my hand over the leathery boot material. The feeling of it made me remember putting on my own little boots at my house in Fort Worth with my Mom and Grandma there to watch the struggle. Another sense memory that put the vision of this one photo I had often seen around the house of me as a child. The chunky little boy in his little cowboy boots and hat with nothing but a diaper on as he playfully ran to the water on a family road trip to Galveston. Happier, more innocent times, for sure.

I decided not to buy a pair and left before I could invest any more emotions into my first stop in town. I was only three minutes in, and I was already having crazy flashbacks from all the things that I thought I had forgotten. This was definitely going to be an interesting trip, I could feel it already.

I grabbed my bag at the carousel and headed to the taxi zone to wait for an Uber. I had booked a week-long stay at a Suites Hotel within walking distance of downtown Fort Worth, the last place I had an apartment when I lived in Texas. I wanted this experience to feel like I was picking up where I left off in a way. But this time, I was there as the best version of myself, confident and ready to face my fears. All of them.

The Uber picked me up, and we drove away from the Dallas Love Field airport. Looking forward down the highway, I knew there was no turning back now.

The long stretches of road seemed so unknown but, at the same time, so familiar. The highway signs, the names of the exits, and the occasional buildings I passed started to all come back to me as the ride went on. Highway 183 took the vehicle right through Hurst, Texas, and I had flashbacks when we passed my high school.

L.D. Bell High School. Wow, what to say about that place? I went through so much during my time there. Not just the normal school dramas, dances, choir performances, friendships, and dating, but some really dark moments in my life played out in those halls, too. There was light in those halls, as well.

After the bleakest, most dramatic events, it was beautiful to see how people rallied around me in those moments. After I was brutally attacked and almost died my senior year, I remember getting cards and a big poster brought to me in the ICU from kids in my classes. And after my mother passed away, just a few months before graduation, I remember the overwhelming love and support my fellow students showed me. I hoped those positive vibes still existed for me now, years into the future.

I shuffled through my handy messenger bag to find my iPhone so I could give my old pal Michael a text to let him know I had arrived. Our friendship had blossomed back to the splendor of its past glory after we had reconnected through a long time mutual friend named April. She found me on Facebook and asked me for some guidance on traversing the shelter system and giving her my advice happened to be inspiring for me, too.

She also asked if I had Michael's number and that one question brought them together in an amazing way but also allowed me the chance to make amends with one of my dearest and lifelong friends. Once we were talking again, he became an integral part in helping me learn my lines for my first off-Broadway show, and our bond was stronger than ever before in a new and beautiful way. My sobriety paved the way for that, and I am forever grateful I found my way to my true path when I did. I was looking forward to seeing my old pal more than I even thought possible.

I sent him a message: "I have arrived! Meet me downtown for a 'drink' and some food?"

I used quotes around drink because he knew my choice of beverages these days would be a non-alcoholic beer or a tonic with lime. People always ask me how I can go to bars or how I could have been a bartender when I am living a sober life. My life's rule since surviving the New York City homeless shelter system has been to look your enemies in the face and say, "You have no power over me anymore."

Once I started following that motto, I found that liquor really did no longer have power over me. I was happy that some people could drink responsibly, but for me, that was never an option. I was a drink-to-get-drunk kind of alcoholic, a half-bottle of vodka in the morning kind of alcoholic. I thought I had all these "reasons" to drink... losing my mother so young, my father being sent to jail when I was even younger, my grandmother's death... the list of reasons went on and on. But when I got sober, I realized they weren't reasons. They were excuses. Excuses to avoid dealing with the actual pain and emotions these traumatic life events brought on.

I was able to deal with the darkness when I let go of my addictions and, most importantly, when I let go of the excuses. The pain was still there, but it was manageable, and I was able to work through the issues. And now, when I have a bad day, instead of turning to a crack pipe or a bottle of whiskey, I let the emotions flow through me and try to find a solution to the problems. It has been working so far.

"We'll meet you at your hotel in thirty minutes," he responded.

I felt a burst of good energy flow through me when I received that text. I was finally back home in Texas, and my best friend from the good old days would be there to meet me. I hoped it would feel like no time had passed. And wait, did he say, "we?"

The Uber pulled into the curved driveway of the Suites Inn in downtown Fort Worth around 2 pm. The hotel looked very classy from the outside and quite spacious. The bright brick exterior and large entryway seemed to welcome me with open arms. As I walked in, I saw a giant Christmas tree, all lit up, and sounds of holiday music playing on the overhead speaker. There was a comforting waft of coffee scent coming from the back side of the lobby, and instantly, I felt good about my decision to stay there.

The woman who greeted me at the front desk also made me feel good about that decision! She was young, of average build, mousy brown hair, with brown eyes, glasses, and the biggest smile on her face. Jessica was as Texan as they come. "Howdy! Welcome to the Suites Inn. Here to celebrate the holidays with us?"

Celebrate the holidays?

I hadn't even thought much about Christmas in the past few years. Not with family, at least. The year before, I was making food with Clarke at my apartment in the Bronx, and the year prior to that, I was "cele-brating" Christmas in a homeless shelter by spending my last couple of bucks to get a star for the tree. I was also cooking with Clarke then, too. Haha.

But as much of "family" as he is and people like Tim and Lacy are to me... they aren't my blood relatives. I hadn't spent a holiday with "real" family in over a decade. And honestly, I didn't know if I would get to this year either. I hadn't really made any set plans, as I just wanted to see where the Universe decided to lead me. It worked out pretty well when I went back to LA for the first time! Who could have imagined that run-in with Justin Bieber?

"Well, technically, I'm here for a book signing, but I think I will be seeing some family while I'm here, for sure," I replied, almost wondering out loud as I answered her.

"Book signing?! Are you an author? What kind of book?" She asked very inquisitively.

I gave her the same answer I gave the airport agent before my last big trip, "My life. The last three years. Hollywood, love, heartbreak, drugs, booze, rock stars, New York, homeless shelters, ego, sobriety, change and dreams finally fulfilled. In a nutshell."

Her response struck a sweetly similar chord to the

comments I got from just about everyone I told my story, a beautiful broken record I could never get tired of hearing. "Wow, that is just so inspiring! I thought about writing a book and just never could get started. But maybe I will. Oh, here's your room key. Take the elevator up to the second floor, and you will be in room 212. Enjoy your stay!"

212.

There was that number again. The last time I stayed in a room with that number was the first homeless shelter I lived at in Manhattan. Back then, 212 was the beginning of my biggest life-changing journey ever, one that was filled with the unknown and unexpected. This day in the hotel was also a new beginning of sorts, and it was definitely not scarce on the unknown and unexpected, as I would soon find out.

I rolled my big suitcase to the gold-plated elevator and arrived at the door to my room within minutes. When I stepped in, I was kind of shocked to see how big it was! It was set up like a studio apartment, complete with the usual hotel amenities but a kitchen and dinner table, too. I could definitely see this being a comfortable home base for the week of adventure that lay ahead.

The bed was so big! And it was so ridiculously comfortable looking that I had to fight the urge to just collapse on it and nap for a while. No, I had to get cleaned up and meet up with one of my oldest friends in the city I once called home.

I walked into the large bathroom with its faux marble countertop, pristinely white tiled wall, and a lovely lighted mirror that illuminated my reflection. I glanced over at myself to fix my hair a little and took a second to breathe. I was finally back in my home state. Blocks away from my last apartment, where so many crazy adventures happened.

Relationships and friendships. Drinks and drugs. All the memories seemed more innocent now for some reason, but maybe it was because I had grown so much since the last time I had been here. Those experiences seemed like child's play in contrast to the struggles I lived through in New York; the year and a half in the shelters made me more open-minded and strong.

"We're in the lobby," a text from Michael read, flashing across my screen while the phone vibrated.

This was it. It was time to face my first Texas fear: actually going out into my old world and seeing how the new me would feel in it. I guess a small part of me, that kid who grew up here, was afraid that someone would notice I was gay and berate me or attack me like in the past. My logical mind knew that Fort

Worth was a pretty progressive town and that it had been over thirteen years - but that younger version of myself was still slightly nervous.

The elevator reached the bottom floor, and when the doors opened, I saw my old friend, and the fears subsided. Michael and I walked briskly toward each other and embraced in a long overdue hug. Thanks to our newly revived friendship, the memories of the last time we physically saw each other during my LA eviction were erased and now replaced with a fresh start. It made me so unbelievably happy to see him.

I gave April a big hug, too. Turns out she and Michael had started dating since we all reconnected and I was happy they had found each other. Michael tended to spend more time to himself and hadn't really been in a relationship in a long time. I was grateful that he had found someone who "got him" and appreciated all his unique quirks the way I did.

Michael was still sporting his long brown hair, but his nails seemed to be shorter and more shapely. He told me he got a second job at a popular 24-hour breakfast diner and was assisting in food prep as well as continuing his job as a masseur at a clinic. He seemed to be in a good place, and I was glad that we both were.

"So, let's go get a drink!" I said, waving them towards the door.

"Shall we drive?" Michael asked.

"No. How about we walk... I'd like to take a literal stroll down memory lane if that's alright with you?"

"No problem. Let's do it," April responded with a smile on her face.

We exited the Suites Hotel and walked past a small apartment complex next door before we hit the sidewalk to the main strip. The first building that came into view was the big burnt-sienna-colored city hall building. It brought back a plethora of memories as we walked past it. Car registrations and such, but mostly, I remembered it for paying tickets for some of my many alcohol-related escapades.

I'm glad those types of instances were just a thing of the past now, but I'd be fooling myself if I didn't think there would be many moments ahead when I would be tempted to drink.

We wandered around the historic downtown streets that were all decorated for Christmas. Either they were particularly beautiful this year or I just hadn't had a clear enough mind to ever appreciate the decorations before. Each lighted holiday tree had its own Texan flare to it, adorned with long-horned bull ornaments and miniature cowboy hats. It brought a smile to my face to see the town through these new, more mentally and spiritually open, eyes.

I had hoped to make my first stop for drinks at a very familiar place, somewhere that was the epicenter of my adventures during my last few years in Texas. But, alas, The Black Dog Tavern was closed. Stepping up to the gate that led to the downstairs bar brought flashes of my early twenties into view.

Jennie, Mandy, Mary - my "Funky Town Mean Girls," as we called ourselves. The drugs, the drinks, the boys, and the late-night prank calls. We even had a burn book of sorts where I wrote down the dramas at week's end and scrapbooked with photos and grand musings from our bar buddies usually written when we were all completely stoned or intoxicated. Those inebriated moments left some very interesting pages filled in the book.

That black metal gate also led upstairs to the parking garage where I smoked pot on the rooftop with other people from the group and also a closet where I had sex with at least one of the "straight" boys who frequented the bar. Oh, did I mention I went to this bar as Sarah Summers quite often? Haha. I was young and reckless, and thanks to my alter ego, I felt invincible and beautiful. I definitely confused a lot of the Black Dog boys in my hay day.

I shook the gate a few times to see if it would unlatch, but it would not, and so we had to make new plans. I took one last look over the three-poled steel fence to soak in the memories of the past. They all felt like such good times, but I know there was a lot of heartbreak there, too. Not just for me but for my Funky Town Mean Girls as well.

Speaking of my old gal pals; I also sent Mandy a text before we left the scene to let her know I had arrived. It had been far too long since we had seen each other, and it appeared her life had changed as much as mine, if not even more positively. But we will get into all that shortly, but first, back to the day at hand.

Michael, April, and I continued our walk down the worn streets of Downtown Fort Worth, only stopping momentarily when we saw an old bookstore and stepped in for a quick glance. I had called this book-shop about possibly hosting my book signing, but when I walked inside, I knew immediately that it wouldn't have worked.

The shop was small, and there were books stacked floor to ceiling on rickety shelves with tiny walkways in between. I was hoping for a big turnout, and this place definitely wouldn't be able to handle it. Another sign that the Universe always knew what was best for me.

Once Michael had his fill of browsing through the dusty old books we headed back out to find our watering hole. Haha. How Texan was that sentence? Our trek led us past a building that used to be another epicenter for my Fort Worth adventures: the nightclub previously known as Vivid. The current business was closed, but when I peered into the front window, I could see that it was still a bar, and the rustic room-encumbering bar was still in its same location.

Flashback to a younger me working for the brother and sister co-owners who were just as eccentric as the bar they ran. I was a bar-back for a while, and I remembered climbing up on top of that long bar to clean the large mirrors and shelves that reflected the glamorous life of the nightly inhabitants of the gay club. I also ran a blackjack table in the back on game nights, which put me at the top of the popularity food chain for a time.

Vivid was a pretty ballsy undertaking for its time. A gay bar in the middle of downtown Fort Worth was unheard of back then. This was well before gay marriage was even considered to be legalized and in one of the most red states in the country. So I give thanks to that duo who brought it to life for all of us outsiders because, for some of us, it brought us to life, too.

I came out of my dreamy thoughts to April tapping at my shoulder and pointing across the street. There was a pub open for lunchtime, and so we headed in its direction. This place served mostly beer and actually had a couple of nonalcoholic options. We all ordered drinks and an appetizer then began to talk.

April and Michael sat on one side and I on the other. Sitting next to him, she brushes her medium-length, straight red hair off the front of her cherub-shaped face. April was shorter and still looked like she did back in high school. Michael hadn't aged much in the face either. They were two odd ducks who were kind of perfect for each other in a beautiful way.

The conversation at the beer bar revolved around my past few years, their life as a couple, Michael taking on a fatherly role with her kids, and, of course, the upcoming book signing at Half Price Books. Picturing him playing *Dad* tickled me a little. I imagined he might be sort of awkward dealing with little people and their personalities, but I knew with all his knowledge and compassion that he would be great at it all. If the kids let him in.

Mid-conversation, I got a text from an ex. *THE* Texan ex-boyfriend who I had my longest relationship with and who put up with all my craziness when it was first really getting started; the one who first introduced me to marijuana and the one who showed me what truly unconditional love was. Shane wrote, "So, did you land? Are we still getting together this evening?"

I had been talking to him off and on over the years. Usually, when I was tipsy, sitting outside some random restaurant and just needing a reassuring voice to comfort me while I was dealing with the drunken drama of the day. He was always so kind to listen to my slurred expressions of pain. It often made me wonder how my life would have turned out if I had been able to get my act together and give him the love he deserved.

"Yes! Looking forward to seeing you. It's been far too long," I typed.

As I pressed the send button I glanced over and saw April place her hand on Michael's. That tiny gesture made me crave the closeness of a boyfriend again. My God, it had been so long since I had any sort of a real relationship that I couldn't even remember the last official one I was in.

I guess the closest thing to a relationship was my close friendship with Joshua in New York. The straight boy who pretended to be my faux-boyfriend leading up to my Sarah Summers off-Broadway show, and we had that electric moment where we shared a passionate kiss on stage and a few off. But that wasn't a "real" relationship in the way most people define it.

Maybe the last real boyfriend I had was the guy who tried to punch my friend outside a big Hollywood party when I was in my early 20s. I honestly don't remember, and that made me sad. Had I been such a complete mess before I got sober that no man would have me longer than a week or two? Yes. I take full credit for being a full-on insane bullet train of alcoholism and addiction. So, what was I hoping for with this reconnection with Shane? I'm not sure, but I would find out soon enough.

The check comes to the table by way of a friendly part-cowboy, part-trucker-looking gentleman. Cowboy boots on the bottom, trucker hat on the top. I pick up the check as way of a saying thanks in advance for all the help they would both be giving me in preparing for the event the next day. The beer and appetizer were good, but it definitely wasn't lunch, so we decided to find a real restaurant to satiate our growling tummies.

We ventured back out into the streets in search of more suitable sustenance, only to find a place that I almost couldn't believe was still in business: Uno's Pizzeria. The reason I was shocked was because I worked there, too, for a very brief time over a decade prior. It was like time had frozen in this one part of downtown, and it was surprisingly nice to feel like some things hadn't changed that much. Maybe my old world really did move on without me, but at least a few things from my personal past still remained.

We all sat at a table by the window, which looked out onto the street I used to navigate home most nights. I vaguely remember my balancing act as I stumbled down the asphalt pathway toward my apartment building. I guess fuzzy memories are better than no memories at all. The daylight renewed my clarity about how far I had come in the many years since I had been there. It was comforting.

We ordered lunch and talked more about the past. Those discussions got me curious about a few other people from my past, and while Michael and April were eating, I decided to open up my Grindr app to see if any of my old gay guy friends were around. The first message I got was from one of those people, and the conversation was definitely intriguing.

Although I didn't recognize his face immediately, and since our screen names didn't grant much assistance, it was up to words to remind me who he was. His sultry half-naked picture with six-pack abs and barely there face didn't give much help either, but it did intrigue me. His first words to me were, "You look so familiar… are you from here?"

"I lived here for a long time when I was younger, and if you were out at the gay clubs, I'm sure we know each other," I responded, hoping it was an old friend I had forgotten about.

He sent me a picture of his face, and then some vague memories popped into my head. Drinking, some drugs, and a few sexual encounters littered my visions. Hmmm, this could be interesting. It had been over a year and a half since I got intimate with anyone, so maybe a Texas hookup with an old acquaintance wouldn't be so bad. My mind started racing with thoughts of my first sexual escapade since going sober. It was kind of scary to imagine. I truly couldn't remember the last time I had sex without the influence of drugs or alcohol. That made me sad.

It made me upset for my younger myself. It made me angry at my past and furious at all the events that led me to believe that sex was something less than special. I guess when I was drunk or high I let my low self-esteem dictate the sexual situations I allowed myself to get into.

Back then, I felt like if I let people use my body, that somehow it made me feel good... needed... wanted. It's so twisted how intoxicants make you feel less than human sometimes, but now that I was sober, I respected my body and my soul, which I had worked so hard to repair. So this time, if I chose to have sex, it would be on my own terms and completely sober. A first for me.

He reminded me his name was Will, and we texted for a bit longer as Michael and April discussed home life. I ended the online conversation by trading phone numbers and a message of hope that maybe, towards the end of the week, he and I could rendezvous at my hotel. I was excited at the idea but nervous, too.

As I put my iPhone down and rejoined the conversation at the table I couldn't help but think about Shane, too. What if we still had some sparks? There was so much information, images, thoughts, and dreams running through my mind that it was pretty exhausting. I definitely needed that nap before facing any more of this Texan adventure. So, we paid the tab and started walking back to the hotel.

The journey through the streets seemed long and almost daunting, knowing that in just a few hours, I'd be seeing one of my 'Great Loves,' as Carrie Bradshaw had coined it. That was a good episode of *Sex and the City* when the girls discussed true loves and how many one person really gets in a lifetime. I feel like maybe I've had a couple of really good ones in my years, but nothing came close to what Shane and I shared... not yet, anyway.

Michael and April both gave me big hugs as we

reached the lobby of the hotel. It was time for him to head off to work and for her to pick up the kids from the babysitter. Oh, life. It was hard for me to imagine at that moment what it would be like to need to have a babysitter on call and juggle work and family time. It was definitely something I wanted in the future but not just yet. I had a few more "big dreams" to see come true before that day arrived.

We also discussed them picking me up a few hours before the event the next day so we could grab some lunch and set up everything at the bookstore. I gave them both another hug and watched them walk out to the parking lot and drive away. I yawned deeply and headed back to the gold-plated elevators and onto my very comfortable king-sized bed. I took a much-needed nap and woke up around 7 pm.

I hopped out of bed and checked my face in the bathroom mirror. Yep, the nap helped, and I looked rested once again. I fussed with my hair a little and decided to change into a more upscale outfit. I swapped out the cowboy boots for a pair of black dress shoes and donned a button-down shirt with fitted black slacks to give a little more professional look. I was going to meet Shane, and I wanted to look my best. Even though he had seen me at my worst many times.

When I received the text that he had arrived I pushed my nerves aside and decided to face my fear with excitement. I mean, what could possibly happen this evening? Was I expecting us to see each other and fall back in love immediately? Was I hoping he would tell me he was proud of the person I had become and ask me to come back to him? Or would he think that all this was just a phase of mine?

I don't know what I was thinking. No expectations, really. Just gonna let the cards fall and play the hand that's dealt. The time was now. And as I turned off the bathroom light and headed to the door I had a momentary flashback of the day I fell in love with him.

When we first started dating, and I came down with the flu, he rushed to my house after work to make me soup and sat by my bed all night as I moaned in pain. I opened up to him about my wild past with full honesty, and he stayed. He loved me unconditionally, and I think it was the first time I had felt that way. The way I felt with him... that was love.

When the elevator reached the lobby, I took a deep breath before the doors opened and grasped at my heart. How long had it been since I last locked eyes with him? Nearly a decade? Yes, I think so. Then the doors opened, and I saw him standing next to the couch. A feeling of comfort and familiarity washed over me as he turned to look at me.

Shane was a tall guy, taller than me, and I liked

that in a mate. He was cute, too. He wasn't the body-builder or rockstar type I usually go for, but he was cute in that Doogie Houser kind of way. (For those of you too young for that reference... he looked like Neil Patrick Harris.) But the most attractive things about him were his kind, soulful eyes, his big, caring heart, and his delightfully sexy level of intelligence. He was smart. He not only stimulated me sexually (and, boy, was he packing) when we were together but mentally, too. Which is ever so important to me. Lust fades, but a person who can make you think is someone worth fighting for.

He and I walked forward in a direct line toward each other and embraced in a firm hug. "You look good. Healthy." The first words out of his mouth after releasing his arms from around my torso. Well, that was a good start to the evening.

"And thankfully, you look just the way I remember you. Have you not aged at all?" I said, giving him an up-and-down inspection.

"Well, you know. It's still the same schedule for me. Same job. Same me."

That was also comforting to hear. My freaking life had been such a rollercoaster since I last saw him that it was actually nice to just see someone who seemed content, even happy, with their life. I had forgotten what that felt like until I got sober.

"And how's that new house of yours? I still can't believe you own a house! That's so exciting," I said, patting him on the back.

"It's really coming along. Would you like to see it before dinner?"

Before dinner? Well, there goes my thought that he might try to (fake) wine me and dine me to get me back to his place. Haha.

"Of course!" I stated matter of factly. *Sure, I'll go look at my life that could have been. That wasn't asking for emotional trouble at all...*

So the plan was set and he led me out to the parking lot to his new car. This guy was really moving up in the world! It was a Prius which totally fit his intellectual persona. It had an onboard computer screen, and I thought that was pretty cool. I wasn't as impressed with the car as I was with his current state of stability. I was almost jealous.

As we drove down the highway, the street lights occasionally whipped past our heads, illuminating our faces. When his eyes lit up each time it made me remember the good times we had. When we took his niece and nephew to the park, had a little picnic and played with them on the playground. I remember falling in love with him again in that moment with the kids. But that was so far in the past. Maybe it wouldn't be the same now.

He pulled the car into the driveway of his house, and I was already giving him kudos in my head. Nice size, bright Christmas lights outside, and, no kidding, a white picket fence. What kind of Hallmark movie was I walking into?! But alas, this was not Hollywood and things in real life don't usually work out the way they do in the movies.

He took me on a grand tour of the place, and it was very quaint. Clean and classy. Very Shane. It did, for a moment, make me think about what our life would have been like if I had decided to stay in Fort Worth and worked on my relationship with him. But we both knew that I was not the househusband type back then. When he and I dated, my Sarah Summers career was taking off, and my dreams to be a star superseded anything else in my life. Sadly, including my relationships.

We sat down on his couch for a bit and discussed where to get dinner. The first place that popped into my head was Ol' South. The 24-hour diner is known for its chicken fried steak and Frog Fries. White gravy-drenched plates of fried potato heaven, named after the mascot of the local college, TCU. My old school. I hoped it would still be open and not just a memory from my past like The Black Dog and Vivid.

We jumped back into the car and drove back towards downtown. Turning down familiar stretches of road until we hit University Drive. The street that led to Texas Christian University was also the street where I bought my first BMW z3 and the street where I walked to my classes as a freshman college student who had recently lost his mother. Good memories and some painful ones, too.

Upon entering the parking lot, the big "Ol' South Pancake House" sign came into view, and I got a warm tingly feeling. *THIS* was a place that really made me feel like I was home and made me glad I decided to face my fears to make this trip. Another sense memory kicked in the second we walked in the door, and I could smell the sweetness of the pancakes and the comforting burn of the fryer oil.

I flashed back to nights with my TCU crew coming to this place after long days of class, pigging out on Frog Fries, working on homework, and when I was just with the girls... discussing boys. I also dined there after nights on the town and occasionally made appearances as Sarah Summers after a show.

I went there after breakups to drown my sorrows

in syrup, too. But it all seems like such simpler times now.

The waitress led us to a table close to the front window and placed our plastic menus down as we sat. Looking around at the rustic wooden decor, the wood panels on the walls, the brownish-gray carpeting, and the pictures in various frames made me long for some of those old times. It also made me long for the chicken fried steak that I had been craving since I made plans for this trip!

I was half-hoping that my favorite waitress, Elvira, would still be working there, but I remembered that she was an older woman back then, and sadly, she might not even be around anymore. She was always so crotchety and snarky with everyone, but she was sweet to me. It wouldn't be the same without her, but the show, aka dinner, must go on. So, we ordered.

The server brought us some coffee in the same old brown mugs I was used to, and we started talking. The conversation quickly turned into a particular scene from *Sex and the City* that I wasn't quite expecting.

"So, I read your book..."

Oh boy. Here we go.

"You did? And what did you think?" I asked, fidgeting with the copy I had set out on the table earlier.

"Well, I really enjoyed it. Most of it. What you went through was tough, and you came out on the other side a better person. But when you talked about us, don't you think you sort of skipped some stuff?"

I knew exactly what part he was talking about. When I described our relationship in a three-line synopsis, by writing something like, "I fell in love with the way he loved me... it ended because I wasn't ready to settle, and I still had big dreams for stardom." Okay, so that's how I felt when writing that brief summary for my first book, but of course, it was short and didn't divulge all the details of the relationship, including my faults, because it wasn't what the chapter called for.

But I knew, sitting at the table with him right then, it was time to make amends to someone I probably hurt very deeply.

"Shane, I know that it was more than just not wanting to settle and my dreams for fame... I was a mess. Not all the time but a lot of the time. I was young, I was never happy with myself or all the good stuff that surrounded me. I always wanted more, even though if I had stopped to look around, I would have realized I already had something great. I was going through so much mentally at the time, and it wasn't fair to get you wrapped up in all of my personal drama. You were a good man to me... probably the best. I thank you for that and I am sorry for anything I did to ever hurt you. You deserve the world, and I hope you get it. I will always have love for you."

He smiled and thanked me for my apology. And just like in that scene with Carrie Bradshaw and Big, it seemed like my chances for a hot night of passion were off. But I think we were better friends in the beginning anyway. I loved talking to Shane, and he always had something interesting to discuss or some dry, witty comment to make me laugh. But I definitely missed his full-body massages that led to sex. Haha.

Dinner arrived, and I pretty much inhaled my chicken fried steak, corn, and mashed potatoes just like in the old days. And after that conversation, I can see why they call it comfort food. It definitely soothed my raw soul that I had just exposed. The side of Frog Fries helped, too.

I then asked, "Hey, do you want to go grab a drink? There is still a gay bar or two open nearby, right?"

"Yeah, a couple of the ones we used to go to are still there but have changed names and owners a few times. We can stop off and have a nightcap before I take you back to the hotel."

We paid the bill, and before we exited, I turned to take a last look at the old place. So much had happened since I last stepped foot onto that carpet, and now it all made sense. I could have lived a good life in Texas, but I don't think I would have become the person I am today if I had stayed. Everything happens for a reason, and it was getting clearer with every minute of my journey back home.

He took me to a bar down the street, and I was sorta hoping maybe someone else from my past might be around to surprise me, but there wasn't. There was a handsome bartender named Snowflake and a sexy, rugged pool player named Raj who caught my eye. I flirted with them both a little just to get my feet wet and maybe to try and make Shane a little jealous.

I had a good time, but I don't think Shane was feeling anything more than friendship, and I was okay with that. I guess it was more of a fantasy in my mind that maybe we'd have one last go at it for old times' sake as they do in TV shows and movies, but in reality, it did just feel better keeping it platonic. There wasn't that lustful spark coming from either of us like there was in the beginning. Time had moved on. We had moved on.

I finished my faux-beer and gave Raj my number for fun. Big, burly Texas man... might be an interesting hook up? Or just another fantasy for me to hold on to for the night. Either way, it was nice to be flirted with and to go to a gay bar with an old friend. A nice ending to my first night back in Texas.

Shane drove me back to the crescent-shaped driveway of the Suites Hotel, and I gave him a kiss on the cheek as we said goodbye. Inside that single kiss was a deeply seeded thank you for all the love he had given me over the years; while we were in the relationship and all those times he just listened to me talk on the phone. He was a good man. And I wished him nothing but the best in the future. I wasn't sure if I'd see him again this week, but I knew he would be a part of my life forever.

I closed his car door and gave him one last little wave as he pulled out onto the street to drive away. A little tear welled up in my eye, and I'm not quite sure if it was a sad tear, a happy tear, or maybe both. But either way it felt good to just feel. To have emotions and release them in a way that only my sobriety allowed. It was real, whatever it was, and it felt good.

I threw myself down on the bed when I got to my room and just lay there for a moment before getting undressed. This was only my first day back, and I had already been in a Texas-sized tornado of emotions. If this was how day one would go, I'm nervous to see what's next. But only time would tell, and it was time for bed.

## Chapter 2 (Part 1): "Everything's Bigger in Texas" Big Day!

The morning sun crept through the curtains just enough to wake me up. It was around 7 am when I finally rolled out of bed and began to get ready for the day. The plush golden-beige comforter called my name as I turned the knob on the spacious shower. No, Mr. Bed... today is a big day. Lots to do.

I quickly washed the scent of the gay bar off me and jumped out of the shower just as fast as I had leaped in. I didn't want to miss the free continental breakfast they were serving in the lobby below. I shaved and did my daily beauty routine before picking out a day-time outfit. I would have to do a costume change later before my big event that evening.

I hurried downstairs, knowing the cutoff time for a free meal was 8 am. There were the usual offerings of cereal, bagels, biscuits, and bacon, but what really caught my eye was the waffle maker. This was no ordinary kitchen contraption! The waffle iron was shaped like the state of Texas, and I couldn't think of a more appropriate thing to have for breakfast.

I poured the batter from the machine into the single-serve cups provided and then into the iron. The smell of the liquid gold touching the hot surface was motivation to my freshly awake body. As the state-shaped waffle cooked I grabbed a cup of hot coffee from the bar and smiled. This already had the making of a great day, and I hoped this was just the beginning of the good to come.

Once my fluffy piece of bready goodness was ready, I grabbed a few more edibles and headed to the lobby tables. I took a picture of my waffle and immediately posted it for the world to see. It really tickled me to be back in Texas eating a waffle shaped like Texas. Sometimes, it's the smallest things that can bring us joy. And I guess my smile was contagious because the woman sitting next to me smiled and said hello.

"Hi! I'm Annie. Happy Holidays! What's your name?" the cute, older, Asian woman asked.

"I'm Kaleb. Nice to meet you. Are you visiting?"

"Yes, sort of. We have a company out here and some family, too. So, we like to stay here when we come because it's cozy, and the Suites feel like a home, you know?" She said, taking a spoonful of oatmeal.

"I agree. I've already got a really great vibe from it. I've got a big event later today, but I think I'll go visit some of my old hangouts before I go."

I told her about my book signing event when she

asked, and we spent about fifteen minutes discussing our lives. It turned out that she would be staying through to the new year, so it appeared I'd at least have a familiar breakfast buddy for my stay. We finished up, and I told her I planned to go to TCU that morning, and she suggested we take the courtesy van. Ahh! Another awesome amenity I didn't even know they had.

I ran back upstairs and grabbed my handy messenger bag and a couple of copies of my book. You never know who I might run into on this Fort Worth adventure. It probably wouldn't be someone like Justin Bieber but maybe an interesting person from my past. I checked my face and hair to make sure it was clear of any residual syrup, and once I was happy with my look, I bolted back downstairs to meet Annie.

The van arrives out front and the driver opens the door for us with a smile. Once we were in the car he asked us where we were headed and introduced himself.

"I'm Greg, Merry Christmas to you both! Where can I take you today?" asked the middle-aged, kind-faced, African-American man.

"I'm Annie, and this is Kaleb. He's headed to TCU, and I would like to do some shopping around here," my passenger cohort answered for us both.

"Great! I'll take you to the new 8th Street shopping district, Miss Annie and Kaleb, I'll drop you off second. Are you going to look into attending the college?"

"No. It's more of a walk down memory lane; I went to school there many moons ago. This is my first time back in Texas in over a decade, and I just want to see some things I left behind. To figure out if I made the right decisions all those years ago," I replied, realizing what I was actually doing as I said it.

Looking into the rear-view mirror Greg asked, "Why has it been so long since you've been back?"

"It's a long story... how much time do you have?" I said, raising an eyebrow and chuckling a little.

"Kaleb told me his story at breakfast and showed me his book; it's very inspiring! I'm proud of this guy, and I just met him!" Annie said, patting me on the shoulder and smiling wide.

I began to tell my crazy tale once again and was about midway through when we got to the drop-off point for Annie. She exited the vehicle and told me she'd see me later. Then she nearly skipped towards the department stores preparing for her shopping adventure.

As the van pulled back onto the street, Greg asked me to continue my story. And once I had finished he decided to tell me a story of his own.

"Thank you for sharing your story. I had someone very close to me who dealt with addiction, and it was such a struggle. I have a feeling you are going to help a lot of people with your words, young man. Keep doing what you are doing. It's good."

Greg went into more detail about his struggles, but that is his story to tell. He's not the first person to pour their heart out to me about addiction and alcoholism, and he wouldn't be the last. It was moments like this, where two random people could connect over something that effects so many, that reminds me of why I am so vocal about my recovery.

The disease of addiction can strike anyone, but it doesn't just affect the person with the problem. It affects everyone around them. It takes an amazing amount of strength to admit you have a problem and a willingness to let go of one's ego to ask for help. It took me a long time to get where I am today, and if just by talking to others, I can help them through their personal struggles, or cope with pain brought on by addicts close to them, then it is my duty to help. It's also just really nice to be able to listen to people; that wasn't a quality I possessed when I was drinking or using drugs.

We drove down University Drive until we arrived at the middle of the TCU campus. The familiar lawn, still colored with green grass, brought that warm tingly feeling back to my body. Memories of yesterdays flowed through my mind at a rapid pace. Choir rehearsals with Dr. Shirey, my first acting classes, my multiple roommates, and all my friends from the dorms. It was like time had stood still at this place, too.

I shook Greg's hand once he parked the van next to the curb, and he gave me a card with his number on it. "Just call me about 10 minutes before you are ready to head back to the hotel, and I'll pick you up here. It was great meeting you, Kaleb. Thanks for listening."

I nodded with a smile and exited the vehicle onto the sidewalk that led to my past. I decided to head to the campus bookstore to see if I could talk to the manager about possibly stocking my book. But first, I took a selfie in front of the TCU sign to let everyone on Facebook know I had arrived. I started getting *likes* on the picture almost immediately from my old schoolmates who had moved all over the country, and that made me happy.

I walked around the corner to the bookstore to find it had changed pretty drastically since the last time I was there. It might have even been in a different building, but it was still so familiar when I stepped inside. The wall-to-wall TCU merchandise, the text-books, the folders, the pens, and the sweaters all brought delightful memories to my mind. I spotted a cafe in the corner and decided to grab a coffee before seeking out the management.

I ordered a medium mocha and sat down at a bar next to the window. The store was pretty quiet because the school was on winter break, but there were still a few people shopping, and maybe some of them were reliving their past, too.

I pulled out a copy of my book and found the ISBN number, which I would need to give to the manager so she could order it for the shelves. I also took a quick second to check my Facebook and was taken aback by a message I had received during my short stroll to the bookstore. A message from the last person I ever expected to hear from in my hometown.

"Just saw your TCU post. How long are you going to be in the area? Would you like to meet up and grab a bite to eat? I'd like to catch up and talk to you about something. -Houston"

Woah. Talk about a blast from my New York past! Houston was an attractive guy I met at a gay bar in Manhattan a few months into my homeless shelter life. We flirted very heavily at the bar, and he invited me to his house in Brooklyn a few days later. The sexual tension was palpable, and the kisses were intense. He was the guy who I helped get into a wedding dress and assisted him with his makeup before stroking his naked manhood and being interrupted by a phone call from his wife.

For those of you who read my first book, you'll remember this guy well. Bisexual who claimed he was in an open relationship but whose wife wasn't so keen on the idea. I really liked him and hoped there would have been something more. I never really spoke to him after that day and never got a clear answer to why everything went down the way it did. Maybe I would find out now?

"I've got a few hours. I'm going to go check out my old dorm and the campus... so yeah, text me when you are close, and we can meet at the wing place across the street," I replied, suddenly getting a little nervous.

I had still remained Facebook friends with him all these years and occasionally would see his posts in my feed. From what I gathered, he was still with his wife and was doing something in the tech field. Honestly, I don't remember because I hadn't really paid much attention after the debacle of that "almost-romance." I knew he was in Texas, but I thought he was further south. What was he doing here? And what did he want with me? Maybe he was going to confront me about my book and what I wrote. Well, that could really go one way or the other.

"Okay, I'll meet you over there in about 45 minutes. Looking forward to seeing you again," he wrote.

*Looking forward to seeing you again?* At least it wasn't, "I'm gonna kill you for what you said in your book." So, that put my mind at ease for the time being. I put my phone away and finished my coffee before getting up to look for the manager. Once I found her, I was quick to learn that the campus bookstore didn't really carry books like mine, and it didn't bode well for my hopes of getting it stocked. Bummer.

But, hey! My book was on the shelves of the Harvard Bookstore, Barnes and Noble, and a few shops in Canada, Amsterdam, and other countries. And I had just been to Miami the month before to receive a medal at the Reader's Favorite Book Awards. I was making strides with my literary work, and even though it sucked, it wouldn't be at my college bookstore; I was happy with all my achievements to date.

I thanked the manager for taking the time to hear me out and picked up a few TCU-branded items to have as useable keepsakes. I bought a few pens, a couple of folders, and two small spiral notebooks with my old college logo emblazoned on top. Maybe

I would write down some ideas for my next book in them. One never knew when inspiration would hit.

I headed out the door and took another look at my phone to see if I had received any other surprising texts. Luckily, there were none, and I breathed a sigh of relief. After my dinner with Shane the night before and his discussion with me about how I portrayed him in my book, I could only imagine what Houston would have to say. My mind went in multiple directions with all the possible outcomes of the impending conversation.

Walking across the school lawn, a funny vision of the past popped into my mind. It was on this same path that two fellow students approached me one afternoon between classes holding a magazine with my picture on the cover and asking for an autograph. The periodical they carried was the *TCU Image*; the college's quarterly magazine that featured school news and articles about student life. That particular quarter, it was my alter ego, Sarah Summers, who adorned the cover, and, believe me, it stirred up a lot of drama.

Having a female illusionist, or drag queen, on the cover of a Christian college's quarterly magazine was groundbreaking in so many ways. I felt honored when the editor, who was in the music program with me, came to me about running an article on my life. She convinced me that a near-death attack in high school, my mother's death, and my newfound love of dressing like a woman and performing as her on stage, would definitely make for an inspiring feature in the magazine. I agreed.

The article received jeers and cheers from the student body, but I was so proud to be a face for those who felt different. I was proud of who I was and where I had come from, and I hoped that the article would inspire others to be freer versions of themselves. For these two girls who asked for my autograph, that was apparent. It had touched them in some way, and that made me happy.

I continued walking through the campus until I came to the giant fountain in front of the student center. Frog Fountain was an iconic structure for the school and a staple in my college memories. All the talks with my Foster Hall friends and the outdoor concerts and rallies. The spot brought back so many good feelings that it almost made me regret not finishing my time there.

It made me sad that I hadn't worked harder in my classes and really stuck it out to earn my degree... but then I probably wouldn't be who I am today if I had. The regret quickly faded, and a feeling of understanding washed over me. I learned and experienced exactly what the Creator needed me to in the time frame allotted. I was meant to be there then and to move on when the time was right.

And at that moment, I also realized that college didn't have to be something that I missed completely. I was still young, and maybe I could go back at some point now that my mind was clear. I wondered if, by chance, there would be any of the staff working in the registrar's office whom I could speak to about how re-enrollment might work. I decided to walk around to see if I could remember which building it was in.

On the path to my destination, I came across my old dormitory, Foster Hall. Memories of my room-mate, Austin, whom I rarely saw because I had my own off-campus apartment, filled my mind. He was a nice guy, tall, good-looking and ran with my circle of pot-smoking friends. Back then, I hardly ever drank and didn't participate with them when they smoked marijuana, but I loved them like family.

Thinking of him and that room also reminded me about the time I invited my boyfriend Tristan over, and we made love in my top-bunk bed. God, I was in love with Tristan. It was a shame we hardly ever talked now after the events that took place in my first book. The Thanksgiving disaster that occurred while I was still in the shelters where I woke up naked and alone in his Brooklyn bed. He still hadn't met the sober me;

the me who was more like the guy he dated when I lived in that dorm room.

This visit to the campus was bringing back more emotions than I was really prepared for.

So, I kept walking.

I found the building where the registrar's office was located and was surprised to find the doors were unlocked. Could it really be that staff was working a few days before Christmas? As I searched the halls for the right room, I wondered what exactly I was going to ask. Could it even be possible for me to attend TCU again? Would I be willing to put my acting and writing dreams on hold for a few years to earn my degree?

I stopped in front of the office door and paused before turning the handle. Was this a door I was ready to open; both physically and emotionally? Sure. This trip was all about journeying into my past and facing fears, so why not just ask some questions? Couldn't hurt. And it might lead to a new adventure and a very interesting story to tell one day.

So, I walked in, and a friendly lady sitting at her desk welcomed me with a smile and open arms. "Hello, there! How can I help you?"

"Hi. I have a few questions. I was a student here a few years ago... actually quite a few years ago, and I was wondering if it was possible to talk about how I might be able to take some classes again?"

"Sure, I can help you out with that. But it couldn't have been that many years ago, you're what, twenty-four, twenty-five?" the sweet, dark-haired lady with glasses asked.

Twenty-four, Twenty-five? I wanted to hug her! I giggled a little, smiled widely at her, and told her my real age. She laughed and said, "Whatever skin regimen you're using, please let me know!"

"Well, honestly, it's a mix of sobriety and following my dreams... mixed with washing with Noxema cold cream and then using some Pond's anti-aging lotion daily. But I think mostly it's the first two."

She asked me for my social security number to look up my student ID and asked me a little about my time at TCU and since. I pulled out a copy of my book and spoke of my story to her and the two other ladies in the room. They seemed to feel every emotional pivot of my tale as I spoke it aloud to them. It was heart-warming to be able to touch people with just words.

Once they got well acquainted with me, the lady helping me said, "Well, I think it would be great to have you back on campus. I bet your story would in-spire a lot of students, and you might be able to do some real good here. It looks like you could simply re-register using your old student ID number, and you could start next fall if you wanted."

Wow. It was shocking how surprisingly easy she was making it sound to make a decision that would alter my everyday life for years. Could I really leave my apartment in New York and go back to school? Could I put my acting career on hold after I had just filmed my first big co-star role on 'Billions'? Maybe there was another option.

"That sounds pretty amazing, but what do you think about taking some classes in the summer? Is that possible?" I asked, thinking that might be a little more feasible on my current life's path.

"That is definitely an option. Let me see what classes are available, and I'll print you out a list. Here's my info. Once you decide what you'd like to do, let me know, and I'll help you out. It was wonderful getting to know you, and I hope to see you again soon," she said, handing me a small stack of paperwork.

And there it was; answers to my burning questions. A possible new path to take. It would definitely be an interesting adventure living in a college dorm again and who knows, maybe a scandalous and inspiring new book would emerge. All those thoughts skipped through my mind as I tucked the papers into my bag and gave the kind staff member a hug. Before I left I signed a copy of my book for her and told her she may be seeing me again one day. Maybe not that summer, but the spark was put into my mind, so, one never knows what the Creator has in store.

"I'm close," a text from Houston read, flashing across my screen as I exited the building.

Here we go. This was one of those unexpected Texas surprises; who would have guessed that he would be here and want to see me? I guess this was an added fear to my list of ones I had to face to get some closure. I walked around the campus for a few minutes longer and just soaked in the feelings from the past and the potential memories of what a summer session might bring. It was kind of exciting to imagine myself as a student once again. And hell, I better do it while I still looked like I was in my mid-twenties! Haha.

By the time I walked from one end of the campus back to the other, where the hot wing bar was, he had already arrived and found a seat at the bar. And just like the first time we met; there he was, sitting at the bar all alone and looking just as good as he did back then.

His hair was still shaggy but not as long as that first encounter. He wore a button-down dark-gray shirt slightly unbuttoned at the top, exposing some of his chest. I could see why I fell for him back then. As I approached, the memories of his hands on my thighs in the smoking section of that dimly lit gay bar in New York started to make me tingle a little.

Visions of his lips on mine for the brief moments we kissed sent my mind on a trek through the dark forest of my alcohol-infused past. I was pretty sure he felt the same way back then, and if it hadn't been for his wife not being as accepting of their open relationship as he said she was... maybe we could have really had something special. But we will never know - because that timeline never had the chance to come into reality; it only existed on some other plane of consciousness and in my old fantasies.

But I was different now. My addict self didn't give two thoughts about possibly breaking up a "happy home." The alcoholic me, like most all addicts, was a selfish person who cared mainly about himself and finding his next high or drink. The new me, the original me, fought hard against those urges to please only myself and actually cared about other people's feelings now. But it would be nice to know that he felt something real back then, too. Guess it was time to find out.

I sat next to him at the bar, and it took him a millisecond to recognize who I was. When he looked into my eyes, I imagined those same heated moments of passion flashed in his mind, too. He put his arm around my shoulder and gave me a side hug from his seat. Our faces gently grazed each other, and an invisible spark of electricity struck between our skin. Two magnets rubbed together, wanting so badly to connect, but the force pushing them apart was so strong.

"Wow, you look really good, Kaleb. I mean, you look great in all your Facebook posts, but it's nice to see that it translates into reality. It's been a while... how are you?" he asked, sliding his hand from my shoulder down my back as it made its way back on his lap.

For some reason, I couldn't help but look at his plump lips as I said, "I've been good. Life is treating me right these days, or maybe I should say, 'I'm treating life right?'"

He bit his lip and looked me in the eyes as he began to speak his next words. "Let me just start by saying, I really liked your book. I want you to know that I really did feel something for you... the situation and the timing just wasn't right."

Confirmation that my memories during that time in my life weren't as hazy as some people wanted to believe. As drunk as I was most of the time, I knew what I felt. Not just in this case but many of the other crazy experiences I went through that sounded almost too hard for me to believe happened. But they did. That time in the shelters wasn't just a nightmare; it was real, and I lived with those memories every day.

He continued, "I wanted you. Those few times when we were together alone were hot. But it just wouldn't have worked. No offense, but you were a mess, and she and I were going through some things, too. Things you didn't know about. But I'm glad we are all in a better place now. I'm really happy for you."

I'm happy for me, too.

Who knows what would have happened if I had tried to get involved in some awkward polyamorous relationship? I had never been intimate with a woman, and as much as I liked him back then, I don't really see myself conforming *THAT* much for a man. Everything happens exactly as it is supposed to. Maybe our mini-romance was simply a blip on my bigger-picture radar that the Universe thought would make good literary fodder for my future memoirs. Twisted way to think but only the Creator knows the answer to that.

We continued to catch up, eat off each other's plates, and enjoy our beers. He even took a sip of my nonalcoholic one to see how much it tasted like the real thing. I noticed him drink from the same side of the glass I had sipped from. Nothing passes these eyes without emotional scrutiny. Maybe he wanted one last taste of me?

We went to the back patio and had a cigarette while we continued to catch up on the last few years. He and his wife did have the re-commitment ceremony after we met, and it seemed they were closer than ever before. I was happy for them. Truly. He was more than just a blip to me, but that was the past, and it was nice to see him living a life where he seemed content. Couldn't be mad about that.

Once back at the bar, he paid for our combined tab in a very gentlemanly gesture. He also said, "I could drive you back to the hotel if you'd like. My car is around the corner, I'd be happy to give you a ride."

"I bet you would!" I said sarcastically as I playfully brushed my hand up and down his bicep area. I almost couldn't believe it came out of my mouth, but at the same time, my being able to be silly with him meant I had mentally taken him out of the "do me now zone" and placed him into the "friends who flirt zone."

The drive back to the hotel was nice; fun even. He put on the Hamilton soundtrack and sang along with the songs for me. It was sweet. For a moment, it made me think, "Would this be our life together had he left his wife for me? Singing show tunes in the car?" Haha. No thanks.

As his SUV pulled into the Suites driveway, and our

time together was coming to an end, I felt the closure I had been looking for. I put my hand on his hand that was resting on the stick shift and said, "Thanks for today. I wish you much happiness from here on out."

"It was really nice to see you. And I wish you the same," he said to me as he leaned over for a very respectful kiss on the cheek.

Although we vowed to keep in contact, and he said they would try to make it to my book signing, this ending felt eerily similar to the last time we said goodbye; I had a feeling I wouldn't be hearing from him again. Not for a long while, anyway.

He drove away, and I let out a huge sigh. That actually turned out much better than I had expected. No angry words or fisticuffs, just an agreeable ending to a story that I never thought I'd finish. It gave me high hopes that the rest of my trip would produce similar outcomes with the next fears to face on my list.

## Chapter 2 (Part 2): "Everything's Bigger in Texas"
## Big Event!

Back in my hotel room around 2:00 pm, it was time to get ready for that evening's big event. I pulled out my black H&M suit that Tim helped me buy before my big book release party at Stonewall in New York City earlier in the year. It was nicely pressed and looked snazzy with a black button-down shirt and no tie. On the lapel of the jacket, I put the silver pin I was given just a month prior at the book awards ceremony in Miami.

My outfit, like this evening's event, was a culmination of all the major events that had led me to this very moment. My heart raced as I wondered how many people from my past would actually show up to support the kid who ran away so many years before. I wondered *WHO* they would be, too.

I had already received confirmation from Mandy and her husband, Michael, and April; of course, some close friends from my high school choir, Karen, Jeremy, and Devon, my old work colleague from Hallmark, Jen, and my cousin Stephanie would be making an appearance, too. But besides them, I wasn't really sure who to expect because there hadn't been many RSVPs on the Facebook page I had set up for the event. It had me a little worried.

Secretly, I hoped that my Uncles, who completely disowned me after my mother's death, would show up and try to make amends for not speaking to me in over a decade. But that was basically a ludicrous dream; why would now be any different? Because I was an award-winning author? Because I had been on TV and in movies? No. To them, I was probably still that gay kid who didn't fit in and blew all the inheritance his mother left him. The outcast. The black sheep.

Fuck them.

If they weren't big enough men to let all that go and try and make things right with the only child of their deceased older sister - then I didn't need them in my life. And I didn't need their energy muddying up an event that was already going to be nerve-wracking for me. It would have been nice to at least hear "good luck" from one of them, but I knew deep down that it would never happen.

I brushed those thoughts away as I brushed a piece of hair out of my face while standing in front of the mirror. Nothing was going to bring me down today. I worked way too hard for this day to let negative thoughts put me in a bad mood. Today, I was proud of myself, even if my uncles were not.

Michael texted me a little after 3:00 pm to ask if I was ready to head in the direction of the bookstore.

I wanted to be able to grab a late lunch with them and maybe do a little shopping before helping set up for the event. The book signing was in Bedford at a shop most everyone in my Texas circle was familiar with; Half Price Books. It was not too far from my old high school and where some of my old pals from back then lived.

This would be my first time back in that area in many years, and it made me nervous. Not because I feared for my physical safety or anything, but because my mental sturdiness was at risk because of all the trigger points that lay along the path to the bookstore. Places I went with my mother and grandmother, the streets of my youth, and all the memories they held. I hadn't thought about these things in years, and now, here I was, coming face to face with my past. The good and the bad.

Michael and April arrived at the hotel around 3:45 pm, and I met them at their car in the parking lot. Once we were on the road, I started going over the notes I had written down for my speech in a small notebook a few days before the flight. I knew this book signing would be even harder than the one in LA because the people in attendance have known me since I was a child.

They saw me go through some of the tough-est things any person should ever have to endure;

especially at a young age. This was my opportunity to show them that I was okay, that I was stronger now because of the struggles of my early life in Texas, and maybe, I could inspire them to do something they had always dreamed of doing.

The drive seemed so long. Downtown Fort Worth to Bedford; I'm not even sure how many miles it was, but it just seemed like time was moving so slowly. It was like I was reliving every moment that had anything to do with any of the buildings along the route. When we made our way passed L.D. Bell High School, water-falls of emotions poured down on me to the point of almost drowning. Even though the bad memories stood out so strongly, I was also experiencing some very happy ones, too.

My years in the choir stood out the most. Ms. Douglas and Ms. Rexroat, my choir teachers, were so supportive of me throughout my years there and even after. Ms. Douglass was like my rock, especially after my mother died. She didn't have to say much to let you know how much she cared; her eyes spoke the words clearly. Ms. Rexroat, back then, was like an older sister to me whom I could laugh with, but as we stayed in contact over the years, she took on a more motherly role, too. Two strong women in my life who helped shape the person I eventually became. I wondered if they would show up at the event.

It also made me think of one of the classes I actually liked; English with Mrs. Edgington. The class I shared with Michael and so many of the people I was so close with in high school. It was one of those classes that, even though I wasn't a huge fan of reading, I loved to write, and we always had some creative projects that allowed me to shine. I wondered what my ol' English teacher would think of me now? One book had been published, and a second was on the way.

It also made me think of the girls I dated in hopes of keeping up appearances that I was straight. Haha. I wasn't really fooling anyone, I don't think. I mean, I definitely liked the girls that I dated and loved them, but it never went further than kissing and the occasional boob grab. It makes me a little sad that I didn't feel comfortable enough back then to just be myself in public.

I had a boyfriend, though. My junior year. He was a senior, was in choir with me, and he just happened to be the captain of the swim team. My goodness, was he sexy! We kept it behind closed doors, but he was definitely my first real love. We did lots of dry-humping on my bed when my mom wasn't home and plenty of kissing, but I was kind of a prude back then, and we didn't have sex while we were dating. Then he went out with one of my gay best friends who went a little further than I did... ahh, high school drama. It made me wonder how he was these days.

We finally arrived at the parking area for Half Price Books after what seemed like watching an extended-cut mental movie of my high school years. The bookstore looked exactly the same from the outside; same sign, same paint job. The pizza place that had been two shops down was gone, but the thrift store next door still remained. It was like I had taken a time machine instead of a car to get there.

A feeling of reassurance washed over me as I stepped out of the vehicle onto the asphalt. I could almost sense the hand of my mother on my back, pushing me forward towards my past. It almost brought tears to my eyes standing there thinking about the times my mom took me to buy books for school or pickup the latest comic book I was into. Over a decade had passed since she died, but being here now made it feel like yesterday.

I held on to that feeling as we crossed the sporadically filled lot and made our way to the Subway sandwich shop a few doors down.

Haha.

How appropriate that I would be having a late lunch at a Subway before my big book event. The last time I was at that restaurant chain, I was buying Justin Bieber his lunch after his credit card was declined. The story made pop culture world news headlines and allowed me to get over 1,000 downloads of my ebook in just three days. This random act of kindness inspired an editor at the New York Post to write a Page Six article about how amazing it was that, in just a year, I had gone from living in a homeless shelter to buying one of the biggest celebrities in the world lunch.

I went ahead and retold the story step-by-step to Michael and April, who were quite entertained by my tales as they ate. Between dramatic turning points in my story, I took bites of my favorite Subway sandwich. The same kind I had been eating since I was in high school. Ham, Provolone, extra mayo on white bread with a bag of cool ranch Doritos.

Eating this particular sub always made me think of Regi; one of the girls I dated in high school. We were in the show choir together, were partners on a few of the dances, and generally just liked being around each other. She was a sweet girl, maybe a bit of a bad girl, too. I always liked a little naughtiness. She worked at a Subway close to our school, and I would always go see her and get this same flavor combination. She told me when we broke up, I told her "it was over" next to the school dumpsters. To this day, she tells me, "You literally dumped me; you dumped me at the dumpsters!" We can laugh about it now, thankfully.

When I finished the story and my sandwich, we

checked the time, and it appeared we still had about 45 minutes before I had to set up at the bookstore. So, we decided to check out the thrift store next door.

Michael immediately darted towards the book section and April to the clothes. I made my way over to the toys section and was very surprised at what I found. Beanie Babies! Haha. Why was I surprised, you ask? Because those little pellet stuffed animals had such a meaningful place in the memories of my childhood.

My Mom, Grandma Ellen, and I were Beanie crazy. We had all caught the obsessive bug, and it brought us together in such a fun, multi-generational way. We used to go to the Beanie Baby swap meets and trade shows that were held in different neighboring cities. Going out and hunting for the rare ones we couldn't find brought joy and adventure to my mother's normally busy work schedule at the hospital.

It also reminded me of my job at Hallmark at the North East Mall and all the fun I had with Jen and the security guard, Alecia. Small-town fun fueled by the Beanie Baby craze. Those were some of the best and most vivid memories I have that the following years of drug and alcohol abuse could not erase.

On this day, hidden under a mound of other stuffed animals, I found a very rare white angel Beanie Baby bear. I took it as a clear sign that my mother, Ulla, and my Grandma Ellen were right there beside me for this trip back home and confirmed that they were proud of me. I found a couple of other little mini-bears that were collector items back in the day. I immediately grabbed them and sent pictures to my old friend, Jen. She loved the nostalgia and told me she would see me at the book signing shortly.

I walked down another aisle while my buddies continued to hunt for their own treasure in the store. While putting my hand onto an odd-shaped vase, I heard my phone ringing in my bag. I shuffled through my notes and books to find it just in time to answer the call before it went to voice mail.

"Hi, this is Ryker from Company Casting. Happy Holidays. I just wanted to call and see if you are able to work on the show The Blacklist on the 5th of January?"

Wow. It had been quite some time since I had worked my FBI Tech gig on that show, and I was super excited because it was my favorite background gig ever. Mostly because I loved my co-stars in the background actors department and had a great rela-tionship with the crew and a few of the principal cast members. What a nice early Christmas gift! I took that as a good sign, too.

Everything was on its way to being pretty perfect for my event, but I was still a little nervous about the crowd size. I think that is normal for any person or performer who is putting themselves out there in such a raw and public fashion. Stage fright of sorts. But what did I really have to be afraid of? I was sober, I was healthy, and, for the first time in a long time, I was happy with my life and who I was becoming. I just hoped the people from my past would be proud.

The three of us bought a few things each and went back to the car to put the bags away before heading into the bookstore. I had been speaking with a lovely young lady for a few months who ran the events department and was scheduled to meet her before the reading.

When we walked in, I immediately felt the energy of my childhood. The decor may have changed, but the vibe was still the same. A hometown bookstore for all ages to explore. My hometown bookstore.

The first thing I noticed was a poster on the checkout counter with a face I knew; mine! It was a save-the-date flyer to let the customers know of my event, and it looked like it had been out for a few weeks. It made me feel a sense of pride when I saw it sitting there. Never in a million years did I think I would be back at Half Price Books in Bedford to host a book signing and reading for a book I wrote. I let a smile appear on my face and continued to look for the associate in charge.

After searching for a few moments, a plucky young blonde employee approached me and said, "Hi! You must be Kaleb. I recognize your face from your book and the flyers. I'm Stacy. Nice to finally meet you in person! We are going to have you set up over here."

Pointing to a good-sized space located almost directly in front of the entryway, she led me to the table I would be speaking at. There were a couple of rows of chairs set up and enough standing room for about 20 more people if needed. I secretly hoped this would have a bigger turnout than my book signing in LA. That event was a huge deal for me, but this one seemed much grander on the scale of my life. This was where I was born and raised.

Stacy and I chatted for a bit, and I helped her set up a display of my books on the table and in a section directly behind so they could be seen as I spoke. Michael and April asked what they could do to help, and I gave them each a task. Michael would be handling the camera for my Facebook Live video feed and April would be manning the Square credit card machine after my reading.

I was less worried about making money than I was about seeing who would show up and being reunited with the people I had cared so much about. A decade is a long time. It felt even longer to me because of all the crazy adventures and the insane rollercoaster life had put me on. Well, I guess, I had been driving the car but didn't realize it until I got sober; life was just trying to steer me in the right direction. (*Step number 5 on that list I learned from the late-night television evangelical I saw on TV while living at the homeless shelter in the first few days of my sobriety.*)

It was around 7:00 pm when people started to show up for the 7:30 event. I think it was Karen from choir who showed up first. She was a grade above me and was one of my main girls back in the day. Her and her best friend at the time, Siobhan, took me in as one of their own and with them I got to feel like one of the girls. I mean, I still told them I was straight, but I'm sure they knew I was gay, and they loved me either way. I felt like I could be myself with them even though I didn't really know who that was yet.

I gave Karen a huge hug, and we chatted for a bit. When she saw Michael, her eyes lit up, and they shared a warm embrace and spent a little time catching up. It kinda boggled my mind that they hadn't seen each other in just about as many years either, but, I guess, even in a somewhat small town, people can not cross paths for a long time. It made me wonder who I would still be seeing all the time had I decided to live my life in Fort Worth. But then again, I might have been dead by now had I stayed there on the dark path I was headed.

*Everything happens for a reason.*

My reason became more apparent as more people from my past began to show up. The next person was Jeremy, a dear friend from high school who, at the beginning of my multiple tries at sobriety, was very supportive. He, too, had struggled with the demons of alcohol and finally found his path out of the darkness. He had a lot of sober time under his belt and was always very encouraging to me via Facebook and the occasional phone conversation. It was awesome to see him in person after all these years and all these common struggles.

The next person to emerge from the doorway was my old Hallmark coworker, Jen. Her bright red hair and cherub-like face were such a lovely sight after so long apart. Thanks to Facebook and cell phones, she and I stayed connected for many years since my Texas departure. She was there for me when my mother died, too. She was more than just a coworker back then; she was one of my best friends.

We shared a huge hug, and I told her how crazy perfect it was that I found that angel beanie baby, and she let out a huge smile. She felt like it had to be a sign from my mom and grandma, too.

Next to enter the memory-filled bookstore was another fellow former show choir member named Devon. She was a spunky lass back in the day, and I remember we sometimes bickered and fought, but at the end of the day, we were always good friends. She had gone through some crazy, difficult stuff in the last few years, and her strength was inspiring to me.

My dear friend Mandy showed up with her handsome husband and another surprise from my past, Kat, the former bartender at our favorite bar, The Black Dog. Kat was looking lovely and beyond comfortable in her true skin.

There were nights at the predominantly straight Black Dog bar where I would go in dressed as Sarah Summers, and maybe in some sense, that inspired her a little in her journey to become the woman she always felt like inside. If it did, I feel honored and proud.

At that time of my life, I was recklessly unafraid to be exactly who I wanted to be - a girl some nights, a boy the others. I even have a picture of Kat before she was fully Kat, dressed in a wig and smiling beside me on stage at the bar when I hosted a one-off drag night. There was a pureness in the smile in that photo, and when I saw her today, the smile was visible again. It made me happy to see someone being so true to their soul, no matter the obstacles that transitioning brings. She was brave, and that inspired me.

My cousin Stephanie, her Mom, and her maternal grandmother showed up.

My ex-boyfriend, the former swim captain, came, too. We shared a little peck on the lips, and, boy, did that spark up some memories. A summer post-graduation hot tub party came to mind. He and I made love that night in the water after everyone left. Still one of my best sexy encounters.

More people from my past showed up, and it was beautiful to see the room overflowing. It truly touched my heart.

It wasn't too long before one of the staff members approached the table to start the event. I was stand-ing off to the side, waiting to hear my name called. I wasn't really nervous about speaking publicly, I mean, I had done it quite a few times since my book's re-lease, but I think I was a little anxious about express-ing all those emotions in front of some of the people who knew me since I was a child.

They would know the pain I felt went I was to talk about losing my mother because they were all there. I also planned to answer the question of why I left Texas in the first place. A lot of them probably already knew, but telling them face-to-face seemed like it might add a layer of emotion I wasn't quite prepared for.

"...ladies and gentleman, Kody Christiansen!"

The crowd began to applaud, and I made my way to the table in front of them. I nodded my head in gratitude and looked around the room to find a sea of familiar smiling faces. I held my book in hand and skimmed through the pages I had bookmarked and then started to speak,

I read the pages about the day I found sobriety in that last homeless shelter in Queens, New York.

As I finished the pages, cheers erupted from the crowd of family and friends, allowing a sense of security to wash over me. I could see the pride emanating from each one of their faces as I continued my talking points.

When I got to the part about my Grandma Ellen, I knew it would be a difficult moment. I looked over at my cousin Stephanie, my Aunt Sue, and Granny Cole and could feel their genuine empathy as I talked about why I had to miss my grandmother's funeral. I thanked Stephanie in front of the crowd for being there for Grandma Ellen when I couldn't be.

She touched her hand to her heart and started to cry a wave of tears. Her feelings that were pouring out transferred to me, and I got choked up when I came to my final words on the subject.

I wiped a tear from my eye and looked out at the crowd as many of them were wiping tears from their eyes, too. This emotional moment made me feel whole in a sense. In that instant, I felt like I was truly home again, and I was loved and safe.

I ended the event by reading a couple of paragraphs from my latest project, which was currently in its infancy: my second book, *One Week in LA | Two Years Later.*

The event was a success. A really historic moment for me. It was a beautiful evening that I'll never forget.

## Chapter 3: Walk in the Park

The sun once again crept through the slight opening in the curtains to kindly wake me out of a peaceful sleep. It had been another day full of reunions and emotions that led to another night of hitting the bed completely drained. But, it was a good kind of exhaustion because it meant I had faced more fears and succeeded at getting past them with grace.

Turns out, going home wasn't quite as scary as I had thought up to this point in the journey. I had been received with love and kindness, which made the fears seem to disappear. Today was going to be another rollercoaster of emotions that I had orchestrated myself.

My plans for the day included a quick breakfast, then coffee with an old high school friend who couldn't make it to my book signing, and then an Uber ride down to the house I used to share with my mother for so many years. I knew that would be a toughie, but it was also something I felt like I had to do.

The memories that awaited me on that cul de sac were definitely something to be afraid of. For all the good things, there were some seriously bad things, too. I was going to need a hearty breakfast to face this day.

I put on my clothes and headed to the elevator with a copy of my book in my bag for good measure. In my life, it seemed like I was always running into someone who might be able to benefit from the words within.

The elevator reached the ground floor and I could already smell the waffle batter heating up and the fresh ground coffee's rich aroma penetrating the crisp air. Texas definitely smelled a bit fresher than New York City. Well... this part of town, anyway. Haha. More on that later.

As I rounded the corner to the continental breakfast bar I was happy to see Annie's sweet face. She was already glowing this morning and greeted me with a kind smile.

"So... how did your book signing event go last night? Tell me all about it!"

"It was beautiful. Really, so much more than I ever expected. So many people surprised me by showing up to support. It was extremely emotional," I said as I reached for a plastic plate.

"I'm so glad to hear that. I was hoping it would be wonderful for you. Come! Sit over here with me, and we'll continue," she said, grasping her coffee in one hand while balancing her full plate in the other.

I prepared my meal, which included another Texas-shaped waffle, lots of bacon, scrambled eggs, and a large bowl of cinnamon spice oatmeal. Hey! I was on a vacation of sorts - I could indulge a little.

We sat and talked while we ate, and I told her all about the previous night's event. She was really touched to hear that my Aunt and her mother showed up, and she asked, "What about your uncles? You mentioned something to me the other day about the strained relationship. Did any of them show up?"

I wanted to say, 'Those bigoted, selfish assholes? Of course not!' Yet, instead, I simply replied, "No."

I guess it was a sore subject for me still. It didn't really bother me most of the time that I had no contact with any of them since my mother's death, but it all seemed to hurt more now that I was back home. I just kept thinking about how they made a promise to my mother to watch over me when she was gone and yet they failed to keep their word. It made me sad thinking that my mother would be so disappointed in them now because I know she loved them all so deeply when she was alive.

I quickly changed the subject and told Annie my

plans for the rest of the day and asked about hers. We were going in opposite directions today, so there would be no shared van ride, but I wished her well on her daily adventures, and she said the same to me. We gave each other a quick hug and parted ways.

I exited the lobby doors and walked around the side of the white building to where the pool was located. I had seen it when I came in but hadn't really had a moment to just sit and relax. It was December, after all, and the water was cold, but I sat next to it to enjoy the sound it made as the wind swept across the surface. It was a moment of tranquility I had needed after the past few days.

Before I got too comfortable, though, I texted my friend Eboni, who I was set to meet downtown for a cup of coffee and a chat. We confirmed a meeting spot, and I told her I was looking forward to reconnecting. It had been a long time since I had seen her, and my memories of those days were pretty hazy.

I think the alcohol and drugs that became my everyday life during my adulthood must have eaten away at some of the fond memories of my teen years. In high school, I was a prude. I think my mom let me have an *Ice Cooler* wine drink one time, but I never tried real booze or drugs back then. I was the poster boy for *Just Say No!* (I mean, I wasn't *really* on the posters, of course, as my dream of acting was still a way in the future back then.)

I just hoped that when I sat with her, some of the lost memories we shared would come rushing back.

Thanks to Facebook, I remained friends with lots of people from my school days, and with some of them, the memories were so vivid, but with others, so vague. It probably didn't help that any physical remnants of my Texas life were destroyed when I couldn't keep up with payments on a storage unit I placed all my belongings and keepsakes in when I abruptly moved to LA the first time.

All my yearbooks, childhood toys, journals, photos from my past... all of it was gone, and I had nothing more than occasional old photos my school friends would post on Facebook. That was until I got a gift of some photos of my father and me from the woman who showed up to my book signing. At least I had a little something now.

I walked back inside, leaving the solitude of the poolside, to go back to my room for a moment and make sure I had everything I needed. The room was so comfortable and spacious that it was kind of hard to leave, but I knew the things I was to do that day were important for my personal growth. So, I left.

I walked the downtown streets while the Christmas music could be heard all around. I passed the Bass Performance Hall, where I remembered singing there with my high school choir in what felt like such a big deal at the time. Choir was my life, and being given the opportunity to perform on such a grand stage was thrilling. So, it was a big deal. Then a few years later, performing at Carnegie Hall in New York City with my college choir was an even more exciting accomplishment.

But the choir days were far behind me and so I kept walking until Bass Hall was behind me, too. I turned another corner to the spot the little cafe where I was to meet Eboni.

Peeking through the large floor-to-ceiling window, I saw a cute African-American girl sitting all alone with a coffee cup in hand and a box sitting on the table. She looked very pretty. Her dark hair in loose curls and the big smile that stretched across her face as I entered the cafe made her look just as youthful as in the old days.

I ran up to my long-lost friend and gave her a huge hug. It had been over a decade since the last time we saw each other. We finally released one another from a long overdue embrace and sat down at the table.

"It's been way too long," she said as she moved a strand of hair from in front of her eyes.

"It has. I don't even remember the last time we were face to face..."

"I think it was around the time of your attack. I visited you in the hospital. You've come such a long way from those days. It's really inspiring," she said, placing her hand on my arm in a comforting manner.

*My attack.*

When I was attacked.

When I almost lost my life at the hands of of few stupid boys outside the coffee shop I worked at my senior year.

It was one of the most intense things I thought I could ever go through, but it was something that ultimately made me stronger. You know the old saying, "What doesn't kill you makes you stronger." Well, I must be strong as hell now after the life I've lived.

I think I am. No, I know I am.

"I came to the hospital after you were transferred from the ICU to check on you. You were pretty worse for wear, but you still had your optimistic spirit. But, we were all worried about you," she said, still holding my forearm with her hand.

"Thank you for coming to see me. Honestly, I don't remember much from the days after the attack. I'm sure they had me on some pretty strong medication to numb the pain. But I do remember all the cards I got and all the love I felt when I finally returned to school. So, thank you for being a friend."

The truth was, I don't know if it was because of the trauma of the attack or the medication or if it was all the drugs and alcohol I had consumed since then that made me forget it all. Maybe my mind just blocked out most of those memories to protect me. I do remember a few weeks after getting out of the hospital, going to the ENT appointment with my mother, and the extremely awkward pain I felt when they removed two long tubes from both nostrils that had been holding the air passage open while I healed. I remember my mother, with her radiant red hair, holding my forearm just as Eboni was doing now.

I smiled at the girl across the table from me and said, "So, what have you been up to? Whatever happened to you? I felt like you disappeared."

She lifted her hand from my arm to fix another curly strand that had fallen out of place, then placed both her hands on her lap before she spoke.

"I did sort of disappear. I had some things happen that required that I move before graduation. But I want you to know that you were one of my first friends at Bell. I remember cheering with you at the pep rallies - you had such spirit, and you always made me feel comfortable and loved."

She took a sip of her coffee before she continued, "I had to go to North Carolina and take care of some very personal things. Things that a high school girl really shouldn't have to go through. It derailed my plans for a while, but even through the struggles, I found beauty. My daughter."

This time it was me who placed my hand on her forearm. Her honesty was beautiful. Inspiring. But what she told me next me even more happy.

"I'm back in school. I've got a 4.0 GPA, and I'm working on a sociology paper about how one's crim-inal record really becomes a scarlet letter in this day and age. Most people find it hard to get jobs and rent apartments, and most of the time, it leads to more crime. I've seen the effects of this. I've also started my own business. Here, this is for you."

I was so impressed by my old friend and the things she had been able to accomplish. She slid the silver box over to me and I opened it up with excitement.

Inside were bath bombs and fragrances of all kinds. Looks like Eboni was turning into a beauty empire diva! The products smelled so good. They were so pretty, too. I could tell she really put her heart and soul into making these products. So, I accepted them with open arms and a big smile. She had really come a long way since we last saw each other. It was nice to find another person from my past who was making such positive things happen in their life regardless of any previous situations.

We talked for another half hour or so before she had to run off to a family get-together. We gave each other another long, heartfelt hug, and I walked her to the front door of the quaint Texas cafe.

"Let's stay in touch," she said as she began to walk in the opposite direction.

"Yes! See you on Facebook, my dear," I replied, giving her one last big smile before heading back in the direction of the hotel. But instead of going back there, I took a left turn on another street I had traversed so many times in the past. The street that led to my last place of residence in the city.

Fireside Drive and my one-bedroom that faced the street on the ground level in the Firestone Apartments. Walking down the sidewalk the memories started to storm my mind like bolts of lightning. Intense feelings of good and bad began to cloud my heart all at the same time.

This was the place I tried crystal meth for the first time with this gorgeous, buff guy named Grey and ended up having sex for over 12 hours. The drug had a way of making you stay very focused on whatever your mind was set on when you took the first puff. Most of the time, back then, my mind was on carnal pleasure. I was in my early 20s, was attractive, fit, and had a lot of money - sex and drugs came easy to me. But it was never fulfilling.

That thought made me angry. I felt so stupid for all the time and money I had wasted. I was young, and I was still hurting from all the things in my childhood that I couldn't deal with.

I stopped and thanked the Universe that I was in a better place now. And then, the good memories started to come.

This was the apartment where I got the news that I would be in Miss Congeniality 2! The place where I fell in love with a handsome and rugged cowboy named Brad, who used to call me his "pie boy" well before I ever got into the bakery business. The home where I shared many nights with good friends as we enjoyed each other's company and spoke of a world we thought our young minds knew so much about. Some of us hadn't really seen much yet... but we were all philosophers when we were smoking pot or chewing on mushrooms.

As I stood in front of my old building I knew that I had made the right decision to move to LA when I did. My life didn't turn out the way I had imagined when I left the state of Texas, but eventually, it started to catch up to my dreams... it just took longer than expected.

I stepped back from the curb a little to take a picture on my phone and then opened the Uber app to find a car to carry me to my next adventure into my past; my childhood home.

The ride from Downtown Fort Worth to my little piece of history in Hurst seemed like another slow-motion scene from a movie. I'm not typically the type of person to get nervous, but I had no idea what to expect when I arrived at the cul de sac where my formative years took place and where I unknowingly shared my last moments at home with my mother as she was before she got so sick.

We passed the mall again, and this time, it was even closer to my backseat window because we were no longer on the highway but getting deeper into my hometown. Further and further into my past.

As we passed West Hurst Elementary, the reality of the moment really hit me: I was home. I had finally made it back to my roots after what seemed like a century of adventures, both good and bad. This was real. I was really here.

The car turned down Redbud Drive and the long downhill slope toward the park and the street that led to mine. My heart raced to the beat of the tire treads against the pavement. Was I truly ready to face this fear?

I could stop the car and ask the driver to turn around and never step foot in the grass in front of my childhood home. I could avoid the wave of memories that were bound to wash over me and potentially drown me. What was I thinking? I had come so far in my sobriety and in my progress toward maturity... did I really want to risk some awful memory seeping in and knocking me off my path?

Yes. I had to reopen this chapter of my life's book so that, maybe, I could finally write a true ending with a sense of closure that I wasn't allowed as a youth.

I said nothing to the driver and let him continue, and within a minute, we turned onto Crosstimber Court. The emotional wave hit pretty hard and quite quickly.

My house still looked pretty much the same. The tree I climbed as a child still stood, and the bushes that grew in front of my bedroom window still thrived. But the energy surrounding it seemed to have disappeared.

I looked across the street to the house of the older couple who I used to visit every day as a kid to see the lawn was desolate and dead. The woman of the house, back in my day, was a brilliant gardener who raised the most beautiful daylilies. In fact, she bred and cultivated her own strains of the vibrant flora and won many awards at the multiple flower shows she participated in.

I remember going over to her house to help her in the garden and the lessons that were imparted during those afternoons. She and her lovable husband became like family to me, and when I left Texas, they were both still living... but I guess a lot more had changed in a decade than I had expected. I mean, they were older back then, but part of me hoped maybe she would still be there and the flowers would still be in bloom.

But like everything else around me now... it seemed so much less beautiful than I remembered. There was a sense of emptiness in the cul de sac now. I'm sure the families that lived there were wonderful and had fulfilling lives but it was clear to me that they were living different lives than the ones we lived when I was here before.

When I turned back to look at my childhood home, I looked at the front window, which led into one of the rooms I slept in. As an only child in a three-bedroom house, I sort of commandeered two rooms for my personal use.

I set up my bedroom to be more like a living room with a futon and my entertainment center complete with all the top video game systems and games. The walls were adorned almost floor to ceiling with pictures and posters of the one and only, Britney Spears. My intimate connection began with her almost as soon as she hit the music scene, but I had no clue when those images hung from my wall that she would eventually become such a huge part of my life.

That futon couch saw a lot of childhood action over the years. Haha. Back then, though, I was the epitome of a prudish choir boy. I mean, I was dealing with my sexuality at the same time, but even with Ricky, my first real boyfriend, we only did over-the-clothes type stuff. Maybe down to our skivvies occasionally and some heavy petting, but with him, it was pretty tame... until after graduation in that hot tub. Wink wink.

He wasn't the only boy that I experimented with on

that couch, though. There was this one boy who lived halfway down the street that was attached to the cul de sac. I don't even remember how Jerry and I started that preteen sexual explorative relationship. Maybe it was that time my other neighbor had a camping night in his backyard, and the three of us got undressed when it got really dark and started playing around with each other.

When you're that young and puberty is about to hit, I think your sexual curiosity is at its peak, and that time in your life lends itself to exploration. I don't think I even knew what "gay" was back then... I just think we knew it felt good and so he and I would play around almost every day after school and after playing a round of video games. We had to be like twelve? Maybe younger?

But I remember Jerry was the first boy to ever make me jealous! I distinctly can picture a moment in time when I called his house to find out where he was, and his mother told me he was at another male friend's house down the street. I remember getting upset and walking over there to confront him! Why was he spending time with another boy? Was he doing the same things with him? Was I not good enough?!

Turns out he was just playing a super cool video game with him that I didn't have but I'll never forget how it made me feel. My hormones must have really been kicking in. Or maybe it was my first form of love? A love I didn't quite understand.

The other room that I commandeered was the "guest room." It was set up with frilly sheets, beautiful curtains, and a lovely six-drawer dresser that must have been antique. It had a giant mirror sitting on top of it, and I loved it. I used that room to sleep in, and now that I think about it, maybe it was because it was more girly, more fancy, and more adult than my bedroom. Maybe the little diva inside of me preferred that room's decor over the video game den next door. It makes sense now.

A car driving by me sort of brought me back to reality for a moment, and so I took a few steps to my right to look at the front door. I was standing close to the curb, so I could really see in, but I could see my memories just as clear as day.

I remember the door opening to the living room, where two Native-American-designed couches sat, and two beautiful paintings hung on the wall that featured some powerful Native American figures with their stunning steeds. My mother became obsessed with the art and culture of Santa Fe after we visited the lovely city on one of our road trips and made our living room over when we returned.

The long couch that sat against the wall held a

lot of memories for me; my mother using reiki on my headaches before I even knew what reiki was and the homework from all my classes that found itself spread out on the wooden coffee table. But I think one of my favorite memories was watching television with my mom on those couches. The favorite shows of a nurse and her son were Chicago Hope and E.R., of course!


..... *end of draft.*

## Holiday in my Hometown: Wrap Up.

### *Flashforward*

Well, I can't leave you all with just that. It's kinda strange to read something I started years ago and try to figure out why I never finished it. There has been so much *LIFE* that has happened since then, but, let me see if I can summarize the rest of the trip without actually finishing the whole book. lol. (Which will be hard because we all know I like to tell a story.)

The visit to my old house might have been part of the reason I never completed the book. The memories were tough. There were some things that I wasn't ready to share and may still not be ready to fully share.

Things that happened with my mother's longtime boyfriend. Things that never should have happened between a young teen boy and someone who was meant to be his father figure. His daily lessons in sexual experimentation ultimately impacted the way I understood my body and then influenced my rela- tionships (trust issues) and sexual fantasies (revolving around older men) thereafter. As a young gay teen nearing puberty, I must have known what was going on was wrong, but I guess I kept the secret as long as I could because he insisted I do so, it was pleasurable, and, of course, I didn't want to hurt my mother. I had never felt those things before with a man. But no matter how it all made me feel - aroused and confused - he was a *man*, an adult, and he should have never let it happen. And it went on for a while before I finally told my mother. She ended the relationship with him immediately. I don't remember exactly how or why I told her, but I remember her being very supportive. She took me to counseling soon after.

I put a lot of misaligned blame on myself for what happened -- and I lived with those feelings of unwarranted guilt for a long time. I didn't tell many people because, maybe, I was ashamed or because I felt like it was my fault; that I had somehow caused it all to happen. It impacted me so much that it became a big part of the darkness that I tried to cover with alcohol and drugs. But, as I grew older, and I confided in dear friends over the years, I realized that it wasn't my fault. No child is ever to blame when an adult takes advantage of their body like that. It is *NEVER* your fault if something like that happens to you.

I never saw that man again. I hated him for what he did to me and how he hurt my mother with his lies and deceit. But the memories of all those moments with him have stayed with me -- and I hope now, by sharing this publicly, the power it once held over me will further dissipate. It is freeing to share things like this, and I encourage others to share their stories, talk to counselors, report it to authorities, or just do whatever *YOU* need to do to release that darkness. *I have put my contact information on the copyright page of this book, I am available to talk or will gladly direct any reader to resources that might help.*

There were other things that might have made me not continue writing this "book that almost was," ... like the stories with Jerry. One day, after my first memoir was published, he reached out to me to ask why I hadn't mentioned him in the book that was supposed to be my life story. He was upset because we had definitely shared lots of intimate moments in our youth, and I hadn't mentioned any of those formative years. I told him that I hadn't really gone into my childhood much because I wasn't ready to talk about it yet and that one day I would write a book with him and those memories inside. He said he understood. We had a really pleasant conversation and talked about the old days and then chatted a few other times in the following weeks. He told me he was pansexual and enjoyed trying new relationships with new people. He seemed really free and like he was living a good life. Then, a few years later, he sent me a really nasty out-of-the-blue message on Facebook saying that the next-door neighbor and I tricked him into doing things with us in the backyard tent one night when we were young boys. We were like twelve! Maybe eleven?! I hardly remember that night, but I didn't have icky feelings when I thought about it. I remember it as three boys just being curious and exploring each other's bodies as kids do. (*Freud would have something to say about it, I'm sure.*) So, for him to then blame little me and this other kid for turning him pansexual or whatever was such a far stretch from reality that it was wild. But it also made me hesitant to share those stories.

Why would I? And why would I now?

Well, I've grown up. I've gone to three of the best universities in the world, I've experienced so much life since then, and I've heard so many people tell me their heartfelt stories. Their hard truths have inspired me to tell more of mine. Stories have the power to connect and to heal. If someone went through some of the things I have gone through but they are too afraid to talk about them, maybe by at least reading my words, they will not feel so alone. That's what all this is about, isn't it? Helping others and connecting.

And, let me tell you, writing and sharing these tough *things* is also overwhelmingly and wonderfully cathartic. Once it is out there, it's out there. Once the words are floating in the ether, there is no going back... and that can be very freeing for your soul.

So, after visiting my old house and experiencing a wealth of positive and negative memories, I went back to the hotel. Later that evening, I met up with a guy who lived in the apartment complex behind the hotel. His name was the same as mine, but he spelled it with a C. We met on Grindr, and he invited me over to watch some *Gilmore Girls* and eat some snacks. I think we got about halfway through one episode of the show before we were in his room, and I was having sober sex with a hot man while oddly (and sort of egotistically enjoying) calling out my own name, which was his name, as he and I messed around. He was great, we kept in touch for a while after, but it wasn't like I was going to move back to Texas for a relationship. Or for *ANY* reason, honestly.

The following day, Christmas Eve, the day I spent with my entire family when I was young and my mother was still alive, I sent a Facebook message to my three uncles:

Uncle S****, Uncle T****, and Uncle R***.
I just wanted to say, 'hello' and Merry Christmas. I went by my old house yesterday, the one I shared with my mother, and I thought about our Christmas pasts. I remember having dinner together at that house with my Grandma Ellen, My mommy, my cousins, and my uncles, who, at one point, I knew loved me. Since it is Christmas and I am in town, I thought now would be the perfect time to reach out and say that I forgive you. I forgive you for not calling me or supporting me for all these years since my mother died. Now that I am older, I understand that when she died, you all were hurting, too. She was your older and only sister. Maybe seeing me made you realize even more that she is gone. Unfortunately, she is. And as much as I have

prayed and wished, she won't be coming back. But I am here. I am still alive. And I hope one day we can be on good terms again, because one day, I'd like to ask you stories about my mother as a child. And now, only you can give me those answers.

Have a Merry Christmas Eve.

With respect and love,

Your Nephew, Kody.


I had hoped that this message would hammer at their frozen hearts, but it didn't. I didn't hear from them on Christmas Eve, and it would be a long time before I ever heard anything from or about any of them. I still spoke with their kids, though. My cousins. Tanya and Heather and, of course, Stephanie who I have mentioned in a few books. The three of them were really my only link to my blood family, and I guess that was fine. *Blood is thicker than water*, the proverbial *THEY* always say. In my experience, it isn't. With those three cousins, yes, we've stayed in contact, but the rest of the family just disappeared from my life shortly after my mother's death.


My chosen family, *my water,* on the other hand, well, they can't get rid of me.


"Tim" and Aimee, "Lacy," Amanda, "Cheri," "Jane," Kayla, and new people who have come into my life through college are all my family of friends and have been by my side and in my heart since the day we met. Some of them I see more than others, and some I talk to more than others, but a true familial friendship bond can be recognized because the next time you see each other or talk, you pick up right where you left off, and it feels like no time has passed. Even if it has been years and a few more wrinkles have appeared.

I did end up spending some time with family on Christmas Eve, though. Stephanie's mom, my Aunt Sue, invited me over to their party that night, and it was so wonderful to share that evening with all of them. Aunt Sue, her sister Aunt Laura (whom I always loved and connected with), Granny Cole (who accepted me as her own), and the rest of their family made me feel at home. And the food was delicious. Aunt Laura surprised me with some incredibly thoughtful gifts of some old photos from years ago. Pictures of me as a little boy at some of the family events and a photo of my mom with a big smile on her face. I cherish those photos.

Christmas Day, I went to see "Rexy" aka Ms. Rexroat, one of my beloved choir teachers from high school. It was lovely to see her again after all those years and to meet her husband and family. Big hugs all around. Then, I Ubered back to Fort Worth to see Mandy and her family. She had just recently had a new child, and Unkie Kody was definitely a favorite of the kiddos. (Unkie Kody enjoyed his time with the kiddos, too.) Mandy found some more old pictures from our Black Dog days, and we reminisced about the "good ol' days" in which some memories were blurry at best. There were some very clear memories - that ultimately bonded her and me forever. I am so glad I have stayed in contact with Mandy all these years. She's truly a beautiful soul.

The next day, it was time to go back to my New York life. That morning, at the hotel, my high school friends Josh (the one who "stole" my boyfriend), Siobhan, and her mother. We all shared some of the breakfast buffet and caught up on the years that had flown by since we last saw each other. I, of course, made some jokes to Josh about the man stealing ... but, they were just that ... jokes. I had come a long way since my high school days. That morning, among the Texas-shaped waffles and scrambled egg plates, I felt a relief. I was with dear old friends and was leaving my hometown that day, having come back to face my fears and achieving that goal.

Mandy, dear Mandy, came to pick me up at the hotel to take me to that airport. The ride was bittersweet. When would we see each other again? It had been so long since I had been back in Texas. There wasn't really much for me there anymore. I mean, the TCU idea - going back to college without having to reapply - sounded like a good plan, but not one that really made sense for where my life was heading. I was just beginning my acting career and had started working on "The Blacklist" and other TV shows. Was finally finishing college in Texas going to put the brakes on that? Probably not. (But we all know that another college -- or three -- did make it into the grand plan eventually.)

As I got out of the car and gave Mandy a long, long hug, I thought to myself, "Well, that wasn't so bad." *No, not the hug. The hug was GREAT!* But the whole trip. I came, I saw, I conquered. And Texas wasn't as scary as I remembered. *Maybe Texas had grown up a little, too.* I said a tearful and grateful goodbye and then headed into the DFW airport. I stopped by the Whataburger to grab a taste of nostalgia before heading to the gate.

I made it back to New York City in time to share some of the end of Hanukkah with Kayla and my French Momma Catherine and the Parigot family. On the last day of that year, I was helping the Parigot team take down the paintings and decorations and pack up the restaurant. The French cafe where a lot of my personal transformation had occurred my first few years in New York was now closed. Good memories, tough memories, and lots of LOVE were centered in that place. I made *family* there.

But as one door closes, another inevitably opens.

The calendar flipped. The Earth completed its rotation.

My first book was on the shelves of Barnes & Noble in NYC and Los Angeles ... and I decided to try living bicoastal.
The doors swung open.
But I haven't been back for another holiday in my hometown.

Yet.

CITY OF
HURST • TEXAS
Library
North East Mall
Senior Center
Recreation Center
HOLIDAY IN MY HOMETOWN

THANK YOU FOR YOUR FRIENDSHIP
THANK YOU FOR YOUR FRIENDSHIP

KODAK PORTRA 400
47
R.H. FOSTER H
EXIT
MESSED
OL'SOUTH

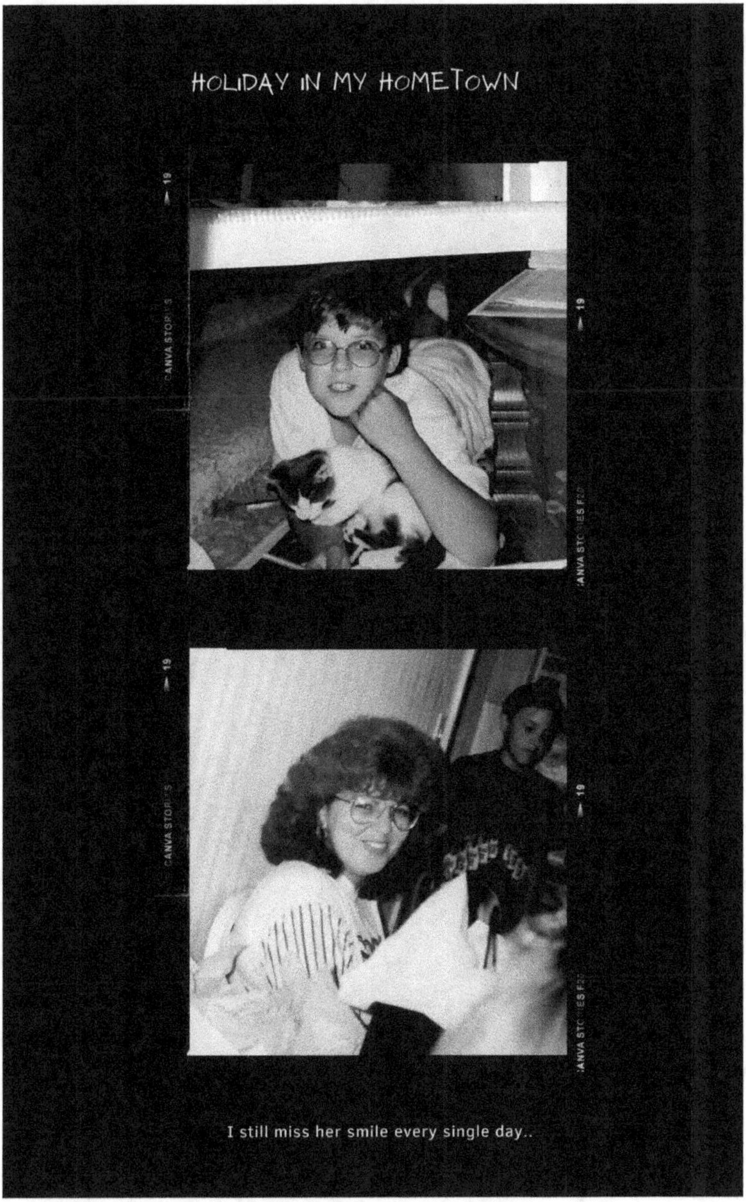

HOLIDAY IN MY HOMETOWN
I still miss her smile every single day..

# Chapter 2

# The Book That Might Still Be

**The Sarah Summers Diary**

## The Sarah Summers Diary
## Prologue

### The First Time We Met

My name is Kaleb, and I am a young man currently living in New York City. I haven't always lived here, though. I was raised in Fort Worth, Texas, and spent many years of my young adult life in Hollywood, California. But it was in North Richland Hills, Texas where I experienced the beginning of my life and the place where I first met Sarah Summers.

Life in Texas was no cakewalk by any means, but I don't think I'd have it any other way. My parents divorced when I was very young, and I don't even remember the time I lived with them as a couple. It was just me, my mother, and my cat Squealer. My mother was a beautiful, fiery red-headed woman of average height and build but I think, when my parents got divorced, is when she started to put on weight. She was pretty big those first few years of my life, slightly obese, but she eventually lost the weight. She worked her tail to the bone as a Registered Nurse for the biggest hospital in the city. So we got along fine. As an only child, I was spoiled, too, but it wasn't all roses and rainbows. I was probably a tough kid to raise alone.

I was very creative and very rambunctious, which led to multiple daily outbursts. I was a star from the very beginning, and I made sure everyone knew it.

I remember it like it was yesterday. The day I met Sarah. I was 5 or 6 years old and had just started kindergarten. The sun was shining through the blinds into my mother's bedroom, situated at the back of our quaint duplex on Crosstimbers Lane.

Visions of my life back then flash into my mind and I remember the house sat on a street that was set back a bit from the main road. There was a large grassy field that stretched far and wide behind the long row of duplexes. Across the street were more duplexes, and just down the road, within walking distance, was our elementary school. It wasn't completely a country bumpkin type setting, it was actually a newer development in the growing community.

Our side of the duplex was always kept up pretty well, which was kind of a miracle because my mother worked so many hours each week. As you walked into our half of the house, the living room greeted you with open arms. I remember the long light blue couch that sat in front of the street-facing window. I remember standing on those cushions for hours, peeking through the blinds, waiting for my father, who promised he would come to spend time with me. He rarely kept his promises.

My grey tabby, Squealer, who I named for his relentless meows as a kitten, was always there to comfort me when my dad didn't show up. He was moody, too, like most cats, but he was a good friend to have when I felt alone. Which I often did.

I didn't mind playing alone in my room. My imagination was wild, and the stories that I would tell with my toys seemed so dramatic and realistic at the time. I was in my own magical world, where the King and the Queen never got a divorce, and their little child, who would someday rule the kingdom, knew nothing of sadness and disappointment.

Another thing that made me extremely happy as a child was music. I remember distinctly the day I started to feel my inner being wanting to come out.

Pop legend Tiffany was playing in the background, as I entertained myself in my mother's room. I remember going through her clothes while she was in the living room resting from another tough day of work at the hospital.

I was always drawn to pretty things and, from the get-go, was a very female-minded soul. I had He-Man, G.I. Joe, and Ninja Turtles toys, but I always ended up playing as She-Ra or April O'Neil. I had Barbies as well. Those were my favorites! I remember asking my mother to buy them for me, but made sure she told the cashier they were for "my sister." Either I was already aware of the social stigma, or I was secretly buying them for the sister that lay within. A twin sister that I would create and become as the years went on.

Sarah made her first appearance that sunny day, in the mirror that sat upon my mother's dresser. Her long blonde hair was but a white t-shirt I had fixed on top of my head, but to me, it felt real. I've always had a big imagination. On this day, I was my idol, Tiffany, up on stage, singing into my hairbrush microphone for the huge crowd below.

This girl I saw in the mirror, looking back at me, would become a huge fixture in my life...eventually. I didn't know her name was Sarah at that moment, but she would introduce herself again a few years down the road. I still think fondly of how my mother handled meeting her, and how my life changed the first time Sarah and I officially met.

## The Sarah Summers Diary (1)
## Chapter 1: The Early Years

In kindergarten, I learned my alphabet and the beginning of the numeric system. It was also the place I started to learn more about myself, and who I really was. My first best friend was Eva. She was a mixed-race little girl who had an older sister and a loving mother and father. We must have been instantly drawn to each other from the very beginning. She happened to live across the street, which helped our young relationship blossom faster.

We used to play house, like every group of little kids did, but ours was a little different. She was the husband, and I was the wife. The youthful memories linger in my mind of the time we spent together in her bedroom, playing with her little kitchen play set. It was one of those plastic Playskool sets that was as big as us, life-size to a child. I don't even know where we got the ideas, television maybe, or our families? Eva was always the lawyer husband and I was the doting wife, cooking up something in the Easy Bake Oven, waiting for my man to get home.

Our version of house went on for a few years, and

one day, even though we were already pretend married, we decided to hold a wedding ceremony. I remember going through my mother's jewelry box to find the perfect ring for Eva to put on my finger. The giant blue topaz ring called out to me, it complimented my eyes so well. I put it in my pocket and snuck out of the house. My mother knew I was going across the street to play, but she didn't know I was pulling a ring heist. Technically, it was something borrowed, old and blue.

Eva, her sister Angelina, our friend LeAnn, and I set up her backyard to look like a wedding. It was really just a fenced-in dirt patch, but with our imaginations, it became a beautiful beach wedding, with grandiose flower arrangements and tons of adoring guests. It was a cute, childish ceremony, complete with a ring exchange and a kiss. We were so sweet back then, her being the man, and me the woman, felt nothing but normal. The way things should be.

She put the ring on my finger, we shared a quick peck on the lips, giggled, and then danced. We must have danced and played for hours. When the sun started to set, I knew it was time to go home. I remember looking at my finger and realizing the ring had disappeared. We hurriedly searched everywhere, but it was nowhere to be found. When I got home, my mother was not pleased at all. I received a pretty bad spanking for that one! You better believe I never "borrowed" one of her rings again.

Fast forward to Halloween, when I was 10. I was set to make my first appearance as a girl at my father's house. I still didn't have a name yet, but I was definitely becoming my own woman. My mother had agreed to let me dress as a nurse, much to the chagrin of my manly, Texan father.

He had remarried for a fifth time to a nice blonde woman with four kids from a previous marriage. They also had a son together, my half-brother, making it a family of 7. When I would come over, there would be six kids in total, plus my father's mother, Maw Maw, making it a household of 9! Looking back on it now, I feel kinda sorry for my step-mom. It was a lot to handle for just one woman. I didn't like her much at first, but eventually, I came to respect and love her.

For the first time in my life, I had siblings. It was crazy, going from an only child to the middle child in the family. Talk about a mind fuck! I had to learn to share and play nice with others. It didn't come easy, but eventually, we all became close. On Halloween, we were going to go trick or treating together, but when my father saw me that evening, he changed his mind.

I felt pretty as could be. My mother had bought me some new hair at the drugstore and applied a full face of makeup to my young mug. Although my blonde locks couldn't have cost more than $10 dollars, it was definitely a step up from the white t-shirt I had used five years before. My mother had found one of her old white nurse's dresses, and we stuffed the chest area with socks. I was still young, so I hadn't filled out just yet. *Not that I ever would.*

I remember ringing the doorbell and one of my step-brothers answering. I don't think he even knew who I was for a second, but when he saw my mom it all made sense. My Maw Maw thought it was cute. My father was not as impressed. While I was playing with the other kids, he took my mother into the kitchen and had words with her.

"No son of mine is going to be dressing like that. No way!" I heard him say at one point. "That's what he wanted to wear! What's the problem? It's Halloween!" my mother replied, trying to defend the choices of her young child.

I always wondered if she knew things before they came out. Before I came out. I can't imagine that my mother, as smart as she was, didn't always have an inkling that I was different. If she did, she was fine with letting me grow up, explore, and come to conclusions on my own terms.

We left shortly after my mother came out of the kitchen, and ended up going to the Halloween party at the North East Mall. I remember it being fun, and if there were looks of judgment, I didn't see them. Eventually, I would come to appreciate the strength and open mind of my mother, but for now, I was innocently oblivious to it all.

The next time I came out was when we moved to Hurst, Texas. I had gained a little weight with the stress of the move, being forced to leave behind my school, the only life I had ever known, and my Eva. I started a new school and quickly made a new group of friends. We were kind of the social outcasts. Bookworms, band geeks, choir kids, and most of us were a little overweight, with accompanying big framed glasses.

I met Michael and James in junior high. Michael was the bookworm, and James was the troublemaker. They were both smart, funny, creative, and talented in their own right. Just like me. We connected over our love of video games, music, comics, sci-fi, and fantasy. Power Rangers was a big hit during that time, and it was another thing that brought us together. I still remember the three of us playing on James's trampoline in his backyard, pretending we were the Rangers. Michael was always Billy (he sort of looked like him), and I was always Kimberly, the pink Ranger, the female lead of the show. Michael would occasionally slip into the role of Trini when he was feeling a little more outgoing. Since James didn't want to be the yellow Ranger and couldn't be Kimberly, he would create his own lead female Ranger, so as not to be out-done by me. We were always a little competitive with each other.

The games would last from the minute we got out of school until the sun went down and it was time to go home. I think it was during these 'play dates' that my acting skills began to shine. It was then that I initially heard my calling to the entertainment world.

It wasn't until I discovered a little show called "Buffy the Vampire Slayer," that I really started to feel my feminine side begin to mature. Buffy Summers was a strong, blonde, female heroine who embodied everything I wanted to be in this world. When I looked at her, I saw power, beauty, popularity, and, most importantly, friendship and acceptance. All things I craved as the young, pudgy, choir nerd I saw myself to be. We played those characters, too. Michael was Giles, of course, James was Faith, and I was Buffy.

I pulled out my blonde wig occasionally when we would act out our own made-up scenes from the show in my front yard. We got so into the scenes sometimes that it felt real. For all the running around, kicking, and punching we did, we probably should have been a little thinner. I remember one night, in particular, we were very into our roles, and there was a conflict between my version of 'Buffy' and James playing 'Faith.' Michael, as 'Giles,' was off to the side, giving me advice on how to handle the situation and occasionally casting protection spells to guard me from attacks.

The battle was so heated, I remember screaming my lines in a rage! The "Aye-Yahs!" that accompanied each kick were yelled with audible force. We were good actors, as each kick was followed by the other person letting out a yelp of fake pain that sounded quite realistic. I guess it must have been one of our best performances ever because we were all kind of shocked when a couple of cop cars pulled up to my cul de sac that evening. The neighbors must have thought there was a serious beatdown going on in my front yard for them to make that call. I was secretly impressed with my acting abilities but mortified that we had to explain to the officers what we were actually doing. I'm not sure exactly what we said, but I'm sure "Don't worry, officer, I'm Buffy the Vampire Slayer" was somewhere in the dialogue.

It was also during this time that I started to realize I had feelings for boys. There was a lot of experimenting going on in those days, and most of it stemmed from the games we were playing. I had another friend in the new neighborhood who I interacted a little differently with when he came over to play. I don't remember the moment when the relationship between Jerry and I went from harmless video games and acting to naked role-playing games. Maybe it was just a natural progression for me, as I had always been a sexually curious child. Before Jerry, there was a boy back at the duplex whom I used to play with. We were next-door neighbors, and he would usually come over when Eva was not around. I don't even remember his name, but I remember the day my mother caught him and I *experimenting* in my bed.

At 6 years old, we must have been playing house, or recreating something we weren't supposed to have seen in a Cinemax movie. I remember he had his shirt off, and I was wearing no pants. His shirt was on my head, and like I had done alone before, we pretended it was my hair. We played with each other, getting a feel for our young bodies, touching and rubbing each other. Curiosity is normal at that age.

During our naively naughty version of house, my mother walked in and caught us mid-kiss. This must have been the first time she saw her child with another boy. She flipped out. She pulled me out of the bed and told us to get dressed, quickly sent the little boy home, and gave me a spanking and a disappointed talking to. Little boys weren't supposed to play like that together.

With Jerry, she never found out.

To me, it was all innocent. It seemed normal. I didn't even realize I was "attracted" to boys until years later. Even though I obviously was, from the very beginning.

Growing up in Texas, I didn't really have any like-minded examples to follow. It was mostly just the "normal" straight relationship stereotypes that surrounded me. There weren't many gay characters on TV, and I didn't even know any gay people in real life. It was another one of those things I would have to learn on my own, unfortunately.

I remember waiting by my window for Jerry to come over, my shirt pulled up to expose some skin. We would play video games for a little while, but it would quickly escalate to removing our clothes and rolling around on the ground or the bed.

He was the first boy that ever got inside me. Physically and mentally. I had reached the age where things started feeling different physically. He was the first, but not the only, person to really explore those new sexual stimulations with me in the early years.

*- end of chapter draft*

# The Sarah Summers Diary (2)

## Chapter 2: Junior High

Junior High. The beginning and the end of so many different relationships. Seventh grade was the first time I joined a choir, and it was in that school in Hurst, Texas, where I found others of my kind. It was also at this school that I would get some of the most troubling news of my young life.

I was in the choir with Michael, James, and a whole slew of new friends. My choir director, Mr. Dean, was a jolly man with a wonderful voice and the fatherly support that some of us kids so desperately needed. During the summer before seventh grade, my father had been arrested and was awaiting trial.

The details of his arrest and his pending trial were kept from me and my step brothers and sister. My father was never really around when I was growing up, but since he had moved his new family to the same city as my mother and I, we had been getting closer and closer. It's a shame that things went down the way they did. I had hoped he would eventually turn out to be the father I had always dreamed of, but that was not to be.

I remember it very clearly. One of the counselor's assistants came into the choir room during rehearsal and motioned for me to come with her. The walk from the choir room to the office was not very far, but for some reason, this day, it felt like miles. Maybe I knew instinctively that it was going to be bad news.

I remember the counselor had a box of tissue on her desk when I walked in. She told me that I would be excused for the rest of the day and that my mother was on her way to pick me up. She told me that I had to go see my father at his house because later that evening, "He would be going away for a while."

As a seventh grader, I don't think I understood the severity of the situation. My innocent nature, my overly abundant optimism, never thought that bad things could happen to me. But they did. This would just be the first of many devastating lows in my life.

My mother picked me up in front of the school, and as we drove over to my father's house, I vaguely remember her telling me, "This is the last time you are going to be seeing your dad for a while, but you're going to be okay Kaleb." Her, my step-mom, and the guidance counselors made it seem like he was going on a tour of duty or an extended vacation. Trying to ease the mental blow, I guess.

When we got to his house, the kids were playing in the backyard, and I joined them. This memory only comes back in flashes, but I remember there were tears. A final hug goodbye before he was gone. I only saw him a few times in prison. Once from behind the glass with my stepmother and half-brother and once across a table in a large cell where we shared some prison-made nachos. A few months later, my stepmother divorced him, and we never went back together.

Back in school, I tried to continue living a "normal" life. In fact, I even dated girls. I saw all the other boys doing it, and even though I didn't necessarily feel anything towards the girls, I felt like that was what I had to do. No one in my Texas life spoke of gays or transgender people, and at the time, I don't even think I realized I was more attracted to boys. I mean, I definitely *was,* but I didn't know what it meant just yet. Innocence of youth.

My first girlfriend was named Jacklyn. A pretty, young blonde who had a reputation in the cafeteria for supposedly doing naughty things with a hotdog. Ahhh, junior high. The rumor mill was always turning at that school. I fell victim to the harsh words and whispered secrets of the other children pretty badly. The relationship with Jacklyn didn't last very long, but the insults and accusations of being gay lasted for years.

But I did have feelings for boys. In fact, one boy in particular gave me the tingles from the very first time I saw him. Justin. He was tall, buff, blonde, ruggedly handsome for a seventh grader, and he was the star of the football team. I distinctly remember the day I had my first feeling of desire for him. I was walking down the back hall of the school, the one that passed in front of the library. There were windows on either side of the hallway that looked out into the courtyard where we all sometimes had lunch. The sun was shining brightly into the hallway that afternoon, and it was like one of those moments from a movie. Maybe there were other kids in the hall, but I don't remember seeing anyone but him.

He was wearing a red t-shirt with our mascot on it with the sleeves cut off and seemed to be walking down the long hall in what felt like slow motion. As he approached me I could see the sweat glistening on his bulging biceps. When he got closer, he lifted his shirt to wipe the sweat from his forehead, which exposed his ripped abs and drove me crazy. "Hey buddy," he said to me as he patted me on the shoulder and continued to walk by.

Buddy? Haha. Whatever he called me, it didn't matter. He spoke to me, and he touched me. I was like a princess at that moment, and he was Prince Charming. I turned around to watch him walk the rest of the way down the hall, and the back was just as good as the front. That scene repeated itself in my dreams for a while after that.

Justin and I became sort of friends. But never more than that. I often thought to myself if I was a beautiful blonde girl, he would totally have been mine. I guess those thoughts had been with me all along, but as I grew older, the desire to actually *BE* that person became stronger.

I even wanted to dress up for a junior high choir performance one year. I tried to get some of the other guys to get on board with the idea of dressing like the Spice Girls as a "joke" and singing *Spice World* for the crowd. The idea was chuckled at, but no one gave it any real consideration. That didn't stop me from dressing up like Geri Halliwell (Sexy Spice/Ginger Spice) alone in my room when I would listen and dance to the songs. Which I did quite often.

It wasn't until high school that I started branching out a little more and exploring the woman in my life. But first, I had to make it through junior high.

*-- end of chapter draft*

## The Sarah Summers Diary (3)
## Chapter 3: High School (Part One)

High School was when I started testing the sexual and relationship waters on my own. I had my first boyfriend, but I was hell-bent on trying to keep my true sexuality a secret. I had already been picked on most of my junior high years and didn't want to give them even more reasons to make fun of me.

I thought I was doing a good job of hiding it. I dated girls. Even though my girlfriends were very pretty and very sweet, I was just never really sexually attracted to them. This was another example of putting my acting skills to the test on a daily basis.

I was confused though, I think. I wanted so much to be like all the other boys. But really, I wanted to be like the other girls more. I wanted to be the popular, blonde cheerleader. When I look back on it now it makes sense. Those girls always got the cutest boys and always had the most friends. That wasn't going to be my life in high school, even though I tried pretty hard to achieve it.

I was in the choir, the band, and the show choir. Music was my outlet to express my true inner self.

When I was up on stage performing, I didn't have to worry about the troubles of high school or the struggles I was facing. I was one with the music and one with the group. A part of something that mattered.

I was very lucky to have Ms. Douglas as my choir teacher. She was a kind but stern woman. She had a look that could kill. If you acted up during rehearsals and if you even dared to mess up in a show... Let's just say, you didn't. Her assistant, Ms. Rexroat, was a younger woman who I really enjoyed getting to know as well. We had a running joke where I called her 'Rexy.' She was more like an older sister to me. Ms. Douglas was definitely the mom. These two women would really be there for me in some of the toughest situations I would ever have to face as a young person.

Turns out I had a lot of very influential and very strong women in my life. My mother, my grandma Ellen, and my favorite teachers. Besides choir and show choir, English was my favorite subject. I didn't always read all the books (thank God for Cliff's Notes), but I did love the intelligent discussions the class offered. Michael and I thrived in this class. It was another safe haven from the craziness in the halls.

We were in PEAK English, the gifted and talented program at our school. It was here that like-minded people were able to express themselves more freely without the feeling of judgment. I was always a good writer, I even won a school poetry contest one year. But I never thought I'd be writing a book one day. In fact, up to my junior year in high school, there wasn't much of a story to tell, or so I thought.

In my junior year, I had my first taste of cat-fishing on the internet. I created a make-believe profile for a girl named 'Sarah' and set my sites on this gorgeous senior named Dallas. I found pictures of some beautiful blonde model and used her less-than-professional-looking images so that my profile might look more 'real.'

When I was this digital version of Sarah, I found my female voice, and with the help of one of my senior girlfriends, I found out his instant messenger screen name. It was amazing the way he treated Sarah. The way he opened up to her. I was able to say the things to him that, as myself, would probably have gotten me beat up or ridiculed. It was the first time I really felt like the girl inside.

When he would pass me in the hall at school, he had no clue. It was a self-induced emotional roller coaster, but I was happily sitting in the front seat, unaware of the bump in the track that lay just ahead. I guess when things got a little too serious, when he started talking about meeting and saying he thought he was falling in love with me, it was time to pull the plug.

If I remember correctly, 'Digital Sarah' had been booked for a modeling gig in Milan and would not be able to talk with him anymore, but she insisted that he get to know her cousin, Kaleb. (Devious, I know.) He was upset. He came to me in the hallway one day and started asking me about her. The twisted web of lies continued, but he was talking to the real me, and I guess that made it all seem okay. (Teenagers! What did we know?)

I told him eventually.

He didn't take it as hard as I thought he would.

Or at least he didn't show it. He didn't threaten to beat me up or tell anyone. But it didn't change anything between us. He didn't say, "I knew it was you. I want to be with the real you," like I had imagined he would. He didn't talk to me for a couple of weeks, though. I can't really imagine the mental anguish that put him through, but I felt his pain. I never did that to anyone again. Turns out, I didn't have to. The real Sarah Summers would appear soon enough and have her own real-world issues with men.

But before she finally came to be, I finally came to terms with my sexuality. I had my first gay best friend and my first boyfriend, all in the same year. Junior year was eventful in the love department.

My first boyfriend, Ricky, was 6'4, buff, dark-haired,

with a chiseled face, a sweet demeanor, and a great singing voice, and he was the captain of the swim team. We were both in the closet at the time, but that didn't keep us from passing notes in the choir room and having special dates at my house. I guess as far as first boyfriends go, I kinda hit the jackpot.

He was gorgeous! I distinctly remember one romantic day in particular. After school, we went over to my house to play video games, but that only lasted a few minutes. Before I knew it we were in my guest bedroom making out, missionary style, with all our clothes on. My mother was working one of her late shifts that afternoon, so I knew we had a little time. We took off our shirts and felt free with each other, hidden away from the world of haters.

The way he kissed me. The way he rubbed my body. Beautiful memories etched into my mind forever. The sun shined through the blinds onto the flowery sheets and frilly pillows and reflected off his muscly back, now glistening with light sweat. It was my first time with my first boyfriend. We didn't go all the way that day, but we got down to our underwear and did almost everything else.

Back then, I was a bit of a prude, a real goody-two-shoes choir boy. I hadn't had any real alcohol yet, just the occasional sip from my mother's wine cooler. And drugs? Oh, hell no! My mother would have killed me!

All her warnings about what drugs had done to the people she had seen in the E.R. were enough to keep me away from those. *D.A.R.E.* (drug abuse resistance education) was also a big program that the government was promoting at schools at the time, which really helped me think twice about doing bad things. I even signed a promissory note at school, pledging to never do drugs.

I broke up with Ricky when I found out he and my gay best friend Josh had hooked up on the side. I think Josh was a little looser with his body and morals than me at this time in our lives. I was hurt. Didn't speak to either of them for a while. They didn't work out, and I kinda laughed it off after a while. I think I loved Ricky, but I still hadn't really felt "real love" until the summer between junior and senior year, when a few of us went to choir camp in Waco, Texas.

It was me, Christy, and a few other kids from my choir. We were staying in the dorms at Baylor University, where the camp was being held, and effectively getting our first taste of college life. I was a big fan of the Austin Powers movies, and my acting skills once again made their grand return, along with a surge in popularity. Thanks to my ability to perfectly mimic the voice and movements of the star himself, I became the center of attention at camp. Once news spread that I could do his voice and actions, kids started coming up to me and asking to hear it. By the second day of camp, everyone was calling me Austin, and I loved every second of the attention.

One boy in particular took notice of me, and I was instantly drawn to him the second I saw him. His name was Matt. He was from a rival school in Keller, Texas, and he was probably the most gorgeous boy I think I had ever seen. I don't know what it was about him. His luscious, shiny chestnut brown hair that swept in front of his right eye, or his gorgeous light brown eyes that glowed as equally as his bright white smile? His tight, well-defined body that could be seen through his tight preppy shirts, or his charming attitude and wit? I guess it was all of it, really.

There is something to be said about the truth of human magnetism. If we are electric beings with souls that emit a magnetic field, then his and mine seemed to be polar opposites that were drawn to each other with intensity. From the first second our eyes locked and our hands met, it was like I was hooked. I wanted nothing more than to just be around him.

...

*-- end of book draft*

# OUTLINE: The Sarah Summers Diary

Prologue: Meeting Sarah at 5.

Chapter 1: Kindergarten -  Eva and curiousity with the boy next door

Chapter 2: 6th Grade/Junior High
Wanting to be the Spice Girls. Father story.

Chapter 3: High School
Trying to be one of the girls - cheerleading. Ricky. The attack, my mother's death. Performing Britney's song *Stronger.*

Chapter 4: College/Village Station
Dorm living/apartment living, Mu Phi performance, the cover of IMage, the queens in Dallas. Tristian, my first college boyfriend.

Chapter 5: Carnegie Hall, Tunnel, life changing decision to move to NY.

Chapter 6: Hello, I'm Britney Spears. World press, NyLa, Ricki Lake, leaving NYC - do I want to be *her* forever? Sex with the hot "straight" guy and the stolen video camera.

Chapter 7: Shane - loved all of me. The Cowboy, The Hustler, drugs and alcohol, performing, Tyra in NYC, call to audition - sending out photos and CDs to fans.

Chapter 8: FTW Mean Girls, Black Dog, Audition in LA ( & the interview), working at the mall (makeup and Hollister), getting the part.

Chapter 9: On the set of MC2, dinner with a producer and his come-ons, going out in WeHo, meeting Derek, the gay porn star, packing it all up, and moving for love. Jim, the blonde surfer.

Chapter 10: My first taste of LA. No big drag scene. Hyatt Sunset. Money dwindled. Drugs in the bathhouse. Started living in hostels. Cosmo Show, Lacy, Paparazzi, and parties.

Chapter 11: Pleasanton, the cake shop. Sarah disappears. Occasional Sarah outings or late-night drunken makeup pictures. Filming the sizzle reel, Britney and Mario Lopez.

*-- end of outline draft*

# The Sarah Summers Diary

## *Flashforward*

This book was to reveal a hidden treasure trove of stories from the perspective of Sarah Summers (aka Britney Valentine) before the heartbreak and dreams in my first memoir. I would have eventually switched from telling it from Kaleb's point of view to Sarah's once she took over my life more often. Which she did. There were days at a time in New York in those early years when I would just live as her 24/7 ... shaving only my face and leg stubble and reapplying my makeup each morning.

The book would have been filled with unshared stories of my past. From *literally* being named "The World's Greatest Britney Spears Impersonator" by MTV, The UK's *HEAT* Magazine, and the US *National Enquirer* to the really hot sex I had with a gorgeous closeted bisexual man who let me film us doing the deed on my handheld video camera. And how he ran away after stealing the camera and $300 from my purse when I went to the bodega on the corner. Little did he know, I took the tape out of the camera before I went to the corner store ... my instincts were right on with that one. But, of course, like all the belongings

I had before I moved to Los Angeles, the tape is long gone -- but it sure would be nice to see how good I looked when I was 19 and living the high life in New York City's West Village.

I call this chapter "The Book That Might Still Be" because I think that these stories want to be told. Sarah Summers (aka Britney Valentine) was a HUGE part of my life. And, although she doesn't come out very much since I started rocking a beard fulltime, she has made appearances in the last decade when opportunities arose. She came out to appear in "A Star is Born" as a background actor - that day on set was amazing.

Here is the Facebook post I made the next morning:
May 25th, 2017
Dear Stefani (Lady Gaga),
Thank you for a truly beautiful day on set yesterday. Thanks for the moment in the morning when you came in and said hellos to all of us and then came right up to me and told me I looked just like one of your old best friends.
Then later in the afternoon, when a few of the "girls" and I ran into you on your way to exercise and you skipped up to the four of us and asked us what we thought about your peephole sports bra and matching tights. And thank you for that conversation you had with us as two of the "girls" shared how your music saved their lives. Watching

you hug them with a beautiful genuineness in your eyes was beyond touching. And thanks for hugging me when I shared that my cake shop made a lot of cakes for you and telling me you "loved them!"

And thank you for the moment at the end of the long day when the production assistants pulled the twelve of us "queens" who spent all day tucked, wigged, panty-hosed, and made-up back onto the set for a final private moment with you. When you thanked us for being a part of this project with you and you handed each of us a white rose - I was left with a feeling of utter respect and pure joy. It made 15 hours in drag all worth it.

And thank you for when you approached me on set for one final hug before you went back to your trailer.

You are a beautiful soul. You treat people with re-spect, and you truly love everyone. It was an honor to work with you. I wish you nothing but success for this film and every other aspect of your life.

With love and thanks,

Britney Valentine

(Kody Christiansen)

Lady Gaga - you embody the motto Stay Strong and Dream Big. Thank you for being you.

The feelings were real. She had made not only me but every other queen on the stage feel seen and heard. And special. It was truly a day I will never forget.

Of course, the final chapters of this book would definitely have to discuss when Sarah (aka Britney) came out during the pandemic to hold a charity event for the Alexandria House: Women and Children's Shelter in Los Angeles. The online fundraiser that made over $1000 for the charity saw me shave my beard-loving face for the first time in years and transform into my feminine self once again to make a new music video to Britney Spears' song "Alien."

The book would probably end on the last time (*at the time of this book's publishing*) that Sarah (aka Britney) came out to play ... at Harvard University for my final film class project. The film "Death and Drag: Britney Valentine One Night in Boston" was a final project for a Harvard film class (that earned me an A) that also won multiple awards in a few film festivals all over the world. It was the first time I had dressed up since the pandemic and the first time I ever really spoke about my thoughts of transitioning when I was younger. The film was probably the most open I had ever been about my female side, and I also spoke about how my mother's death impacted it all.

Scan QR Code to
Watch

Watch the award-winning short film
"Death & Drag: Britney Valentine
- One Night in Boston"

Youtube link:
https://www.youtube.com/watch?v=7oWAoS6XnQ8

So, we shall see what comes of this "Might Still Be"
book. I think telling some stories from her perspective might be something different, and maybe it might
connect with another swath of readers who might not
have a lot of books to connect to in that way.

Sarah (aka Britney) always surprises me and comes
out when I least expect it. So, as always, stay tuned.

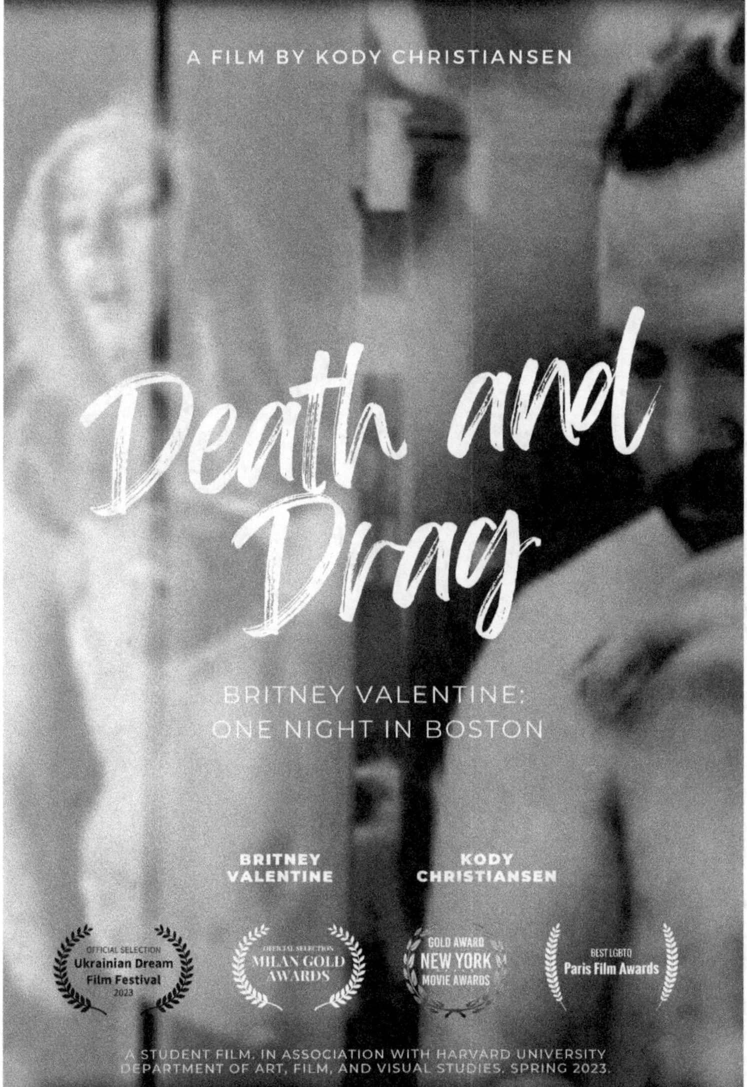
A FILM BY KODY CHRISTIANSEN
Death and Drag
BRITNEY VALENTINE:
ONE NIGHT IN BOSTON
BRITNEY
VALENTINE
KODY
CHRISTIANSEN
OFFICIAL SELECTION
Ukrainian Dream
Film Festival
2023
OFFICIAL SELECTION
MILAN GOLD
AWARDS
GOLD AWARD
NEW YORK
MOVIE AWARDS
BEST LGBTQ
Paris Film Awards
A STUDENT FILM, IN ASSOCIATION WITH HARVARD UNIVERSITY
DEPARTMENT OF ART, FILM, AND VISUAL STUDIES. SPRING 2023.

# Chapter 3

# The Book That Became Another Book

"I am Just Me" or "Me and My Inner Me"

*this draft eventually became the children's books "I'm Just Me!" and "I'm Just Me!!"*

When my mother got home from work at the hospital, she liked to take a nap.

I didn't blame her because she spent most of the day helping to save people's lives.

But as an only child, I found myself alone a lot and had to find all sorts of ways to have fun.

I loved to draw and color.

I loved to play with my action figures.

I loved to read books.

I loved to play with my cat, Squealer.

I loved to call my Grandma and make pretend adventures over the phone.

But what I think I really loved most of all was when I would sneak into my mommy's closet and put on her shoes.

I loved to put a shirt over my head and pretend it was hair and use my hairbrush to pretend it was a microphone!

I danced around in my bedroom singing my favorite songs by my favorite female musicians...

And I think that's when I felt most comfortable. When I felt like the inner me was on the outside for once.

I don't know if my mother knew that I liked to dress up like her sometimes but she always let me be myself.

I'd ask her to buy me dolls sometimes and she wasn't afraid to say yes.

So when I got home, I would play with the little dresses and brush the doll's hair, and I felt like the inner me once more.

One year, for Halloween, when I was in my early teens, she even let me dress as a lady nurse!

She lent me her old nurse's dress and helped me style the hair we bought at the drugstore.

For that one night, I felt like my dolls and I felt like the inner me again.

Many years went by and one day in high school I took my mom out to dinner to talk.

"Mom," I said. "I need to tell you something important. Something I've been hiding all my life."

My mother grabbed my hand and a tear fell down her face. Did she already know my deepest, darkest secret?

"My son, my only boy, I love you no matter what you are going to say."

It was there at the table I spoke the words, "Mom, I think I'm gay."

She held my hand and then came around the table. She hugged me sweetly and kissed me on the cheek.

"You, my child, can be whatever you choose to be in this world. I will always love you equally."

My mother was the best. She helped me figure out who I was. She even kept my secret when I wasn't quite ready to tell the world.

My mother, my best friend, became an angel before I graduated from school. Cancer is the worst. But I still feel her love guiding me on my path to becoming who she knew I could be.

When I became an adult, I could dress up whenever I wanted and made friends who accepted me for exactly who I was.

A group of boys being girls who became sisters in a club.

I even appeared in TV shows and movies as a girl and made a job out of dressing up!

Life is hard sometimes but it always seems to get

better. If you have faith in your inner self and stay true to your desires.

I am free as a bird and free of my demons. I am proud of who I am. A gay man who can let his inner diva out whenever she pleases.

Live life out loud and proud.
Don't be afraid to be you.
Stay Strong and Dream Big.
To your inner self always be true.

personal sketch

# CIGARS

Poetry

# Cigars

The cord is obsolete...
Kody Christiansen

The cord is obsolete
each twist and turn
a rounded edge of shine
smooth and firm
a plastic lifeline--The shell
of the connectors--meets--everything
end to end - wall to receiver–

hello? He begins–

But if he begins
the end is near
words lasting minutes
becoming hours in dreams–

Longing, trusting, more sanguine
anger wrapped in love–
broken promises
transferred through plastic

Somewhere the truth
in linguistic acrobatics

emotional acrobatics–

The cord carried the weight of hope
but hope is not at the end--of cords

It is at the edge of the
mind where kept promises wait

Tired, deflated to resign
Worthless--fragile
sad, lonely, half-grown
scorned, disheartened, disconnecting

What

The galaxy between his words
my ears and the

From that twisted shine wrapped around
that tiny finger of mine
infinitely optimistic, infinitely
disappointed memories
the payphone crackles
another quarter--struggling
to father--neither hanging
up nor speaking–

The sound of his voice
unheard
penetrates silence

______________________________________

*Inspired by "The rose is obsolete..." by William Carlos Williams.*

# Chapter 4

# Poetry: The Years Before College & Sobriety

Poems written in the many years before I ever stepped foot into the classrooms of NYU, Harvard, or Cambridge.

These are the poems of days gone by.

Post-high school and pre-college.

# Poetry: The Years Before College & Sobriety

Table of Contents:

1. Conscious in Your Eyes

2. Just be ... here.

3. The Scream and Shout (Song)

4. Why now - we've only just begun.

5. Don't you know who I am?

6. Lost and Found

7. HANDLE WITH CARE

## CONSCIOUS IN YOUR EYES

Lovers we lost and lovers we'll gain
Leaving holes in your heart, but space will remain
Turning leaves will fall for you - like I do today
Whispers are but echoes of words we've yet to say
Living to love and loving to live
Asking so little with so much to give
Open hearts become revolving doors
And shattered souls scattered on floors
Every goodbye greets another hello
When foe becomes friend and friend becomes foe
But a harmony is not so easily found
Listen close for peace and it's melodious sound
When dawn did break the dark's night sky
I feel grateful this time has not passed us by
With memories like seasons, there is always a new
These pleasures and pain, fresh moments,
my soul does renew
Listening so carefully to my brave little bird
Sweet passion and romance drip
soft with each word
Life is but numbers and stars that cross paths
Your heartbeat does comfort me -
like rose petal baths
The world is so large yet ours is quite small
Billions of people that now don't matter at all
Love is to life what time has never been
Something so physical yet flows deeper within

Sharing this space we entertain one another
Sparking my mind I search deeper to discover
To be one in one - connected through thought
In these moments with you life lessons were taught
Dare not to ponder of what lies ahead
Be patient, sweet one it awaits you in bed
Sweet dreams of fulfillment - an amazing new joy
Life's like a blank page -
today's just the beginning my boy
Those holes in your heart and all of that space
When freed from your pain - my love will replace
Today, warmth from the sun
touches oceans and skies
Nothing but a fraction of the heat
that glows in your eyes
Lustful thoughts do linger for hours
With visions and conceptions
I'm entranced by your powers
Fantasies become reality
like stories from great novels
Life is definitely more beautiful
in this grand city of angels.

## Just be ... here.

I can hear you scream inside
your passion rolls in like the tide
and you feel so alone
but you can't go home

I know just what you're going through
so let me stay and comfort you
you'll make it through the night
everything will be alright

I'm here - to chase away your fears
and I'm here - to wipe away your tears
Put your faith in me
just close your eyes and be ... here.

## The Scream and Shout (Song)

INTRO:
I think, therefore, I am.
I am what I eat
I'm hungry.....

CHORUS:
Ooooh oh yea. Oh yea, oh yea, oh yea.
Hey!

VERSE 1
Boy, do you like it raw?
Boy, do you like it hot?
Eating here or eating out?
Welcome to the Scream and Shout!
We have salads tossed to please
Our sexy staff serves all your needs.

CHORUS

VERSE 2
How do you like it, girl?
How do you want it served?
On a platter, in a bun, pull it out let's have some fun.
Need a side of special sauce?
Hold the phone I'll get the boss.

CHORUS

VERSE 3
So there are 3 of you?
You ready for something new?
Follow me now hurry up.
Candy's here to fill your cup.
Try her big banana split
It's so big your pants won't zip.

CHORUS

VERSE 4
At scream and shout you're in and out
We're the best - we have no doubt
Stay all night or come back later
Just don't hog our elevator

V/O
Thanks for choosing Scream and Shout -
We hope you had your fill
We're open 24 hours kids –
so ya'll come back now ya hear?

Why now – we've only just begun.


Everything I do has to be so calculated
Why can't I just be me and be totally elated?
Every time, I think that this is the best bet
Other people bring me down with sorrow and regret.
Why do I try so hard to live in public scrutiny?
When all I want is love and a love next to me.
I guess my best is not enough for you, though
Maybe I still need time to germinate and grow.
The cards were very clear about my entirety
I give my heart, my trust, my self all too easily
I always think the best – live the golden rule
But maybe I, myself, am just a simple fool.
Hearts get broken every day and no one seems to care
But what did I do this time? This is so not even fair.
I'm in another void of pain but I can't lay all the blame
I guess I was being stupid to think
it would always be the same.
I don't want to leave you now
but I guess I have no choice
All my thoughts, my love,
can't be heard within my voice.
I guess real love is scary and more than some can take
But now I wonder just how many times
can my heart truly love and break?

## Don't you know who I am?

Don't you know who I am?
They say I'm just her number-one fan
But that's not what this is
It's not just about the biz
I'm here to do some good
I hope that's understood.
People always talk about me saying that I'm wild.
When looking for fun it's always
my number that is dialed.
Yeah, I like to party and dress in fancy clothes.
But there is so much more to me
that no one even knows
I'm deep, I'm sweet, I got a brain inside this head
I'm ready to take over – yes, that is what I said.
Please don't get too scared now, miss,
it's all just for fun.
I just hope they remember us both
when all of this is done.
Let's dance and sing and make crazy music videos.
Two heads are better than one, my dear,
and it really shows.
You have gotten oh so far and inspired fashion
trends.
But together with our true feelings,
we'll inspire revolutions
Don't you know who I am?

They say I'm just your number-one fan
But that's not what this is
It's not just about the biz
I'm here to do some good
I hope that's understood.

- Britney Valentine

## Lost and Found

Some thieves at night seek hearts to steal
So cold inside they can't even feel
Villains seeking victims with another heart to break
With every heart a piece of soul they willingly do take

While feeding off these desperate fools
They too are fed on by heartless ghouls
Sucking life from the vessel's veins
No soul inside just flesh remains

Morality and empathy don't ever cross their mind
They please themselves with every new fragile find
Each heart that's drained befalls a curse
Becomes a song with a wordless verse

Never knowing that their own heart died
Emotionless voids where souls did reside
Although it seems there is no cure
There is a way to make the heart re-pure

Listen hard for that little voice
Remember your power to make a choice
Release this curse to reveal your fate
Blessings come when you find your soul's mate.

## HANDLE WITH CARE

Fragile little children playing adult games
Lost in hectic worlds where no one knows their names
Pretending not to notice they shyly brush off stares
They wonder why their book of life
already has many tears

Being in this realm for them is like living in the wild
Running from the predators like a hopeless little child
Some of them they have some sense
and always travel in packs
But those kids who run alone usually
end up on their backs

New you may be wondering what
children do I speak of?
How about the boy next door
who's neglected and needs love?
His drunk mother who left him at two
and his father beats him bad
He's just another "nelly faggot"
and that's not cool with his dad
When no one understands him
he doesn't know what to do
So he sneaks into the gay bar and tosses back a few
It's in this desperate moment
the vultures circle their prey

This nasty older man walks up
and says he's willing to pay
... well Daddy doesn't love me and I AM a little drunk
"Hey old man, yea, how about $200 for fuck?"

Fragile little children become tainted young adults
With scars so deep the band-aids
are fastened with lots of nuts and bolts
Now that you're informed you can't
just watch his life go down the hill
Always inspire, teach, reach out and love
- it can really help him heal.


Kody Christiansen | Los Angeles

# Chapter 5

# Poems from the (Harvard) Heart

A Collection of Poems by Kody Christiansen

Written at Harvard University in 2020

*aka the Pandemic Year*

Course: *Beginning Poetry: Listening to Lines*
Taught by: Professor David Barber

## Poems From the (Harvard) Heart | 2020

TABLE OF CONTENTS
Name of Poem (Harvard Weekly Assignment)

1. The Longest Weekend (Ode or Elegy)
2. No Strings Attached (Monologue or Persona Poem)
3. We Can (Ballad Measure or Repeating Device)
4. The Bum Bum Sonnet (Lyric poem written in fixed verse and/or formal stanzas)
5. In the Stacks (A poem based on "an example of an example)
6. Blinded by the Right ( Poem based on a formal experiment or technical exercise)
7. The First Time (Poem responding to a work of art)
8. When the Bells Call Out to You (Meditative poem invoking a sense of place)
9. Room 212 (Two Paths into the Deep Past)
10. BEEP ZAP BOOP ZOT! (Occasional Poem of Any Variety)
11. Because I stoped for death (Poem taking informed inspiration from a master poet)
12. Borrowed Voices (Revisit a course assignment : occasional)
13. Remember Before? (Wild Card Revised)
14. Something to End On
15. Final Thoughts

# The Longest Weekend

## By: Kody Christiansen

Sometimes I feel good and sometimes I do not.

Each day is different and looks nothing like I sought.

Two years of my life were supposed to be the best,

But in a minute the call said I must sit out the rest.

We didn't even get to say a real goodbye to our special friends.

Digital celebrations remain just some pleasant means to the ends.

I cry, I laugh, I scream out loud.

But deep inside I know I should be proud.

Before the shutdown I was open-wide.

I shared my love, my life, with the big world outside.

Alone in this room for so many days away...

In my head it is for the strength that I pray.

Strength to stay optimistic and strength to stay connected.

Strength to remain focused when from certain dreams I've been rejected.

I don't know what the next year of my life looks like and that's a scary thought.

But whatever may be to happen I will make use of the lessons I've been taught.

Hold tight to those sweet memories until we can make anew.

Think fondly of those times when you're feeling sad and blue.

In a world of uncertainty there is one thing that I know,

This time away from it all must be a time for us to grow.

To everyone dealing with the loss of normal life  - my love to you I send.

Fear not, my friends, for one day we will be free from this extremely long weekend.

## No Strings Attached.

### By: Kody Christiansen

I couldn't believe what was happening.

I couldn't believe my eyes.

The life that had been sparked inside this toy,

this puppet, I thought was something so pure.

But it was vile.

It was violent.

But it didn't show itself right away. No. It was a good little puppet the first few weeks. Being led by the strings and my hands seemed to create a feeling of content for both the puppet and I.

But...

One day as I was sleeping, this wooden being of my creation, found the scissors of sterling silver and ... CHOP CHOP CHOP CHOP.

All four strings were cut in the dead of night.

I was a fool, you see. For the next week or so, I believed his strings still to be attached - I wasn't looking close enough. And by the time I realized what had been done - it was too late.

My creation was no longer a puppet, not even a wooden toy - but a monster of gigantic proportions! As his head and ego grew with his feelings of power, so did his body until one day he was as big as the tallest structure in our little town.

Then he started the rampage.

And I, feeling guilty that I had unleashed this beast upon our quiet town, began to plan how I would clean up this mess.

## We Can.

By: Kody Christiansen

I am here,
But I am not.
I am nowhere
Is what I thought.


I am lost
In the world unknown.
I am lost
But I am not alone.


I am powerful
It is plain to see.
I am everyone
And everyone is me.


We can find
Our way through it all.
We can keep
Each other from the great fall.

Our goal is
Is to finish strong.
Our goal becomes
One and so does our bond.


This is a
Battle that must surely be won.
This is our moment, let's finish it.
DONE.

# The Bum Bum Sonnet

## By Kody Christiansen

In this sonnet, you will find a pattern.
A rhythm that beats as you read along.
Easy to spot like the rings of Saturn,
The beat you see becomes a little song.
You can tap your fingers or hum it out,
Fear not, you catch on eventually.
Like a teapot with a hot steaming spout,
The downbeat comes along so sneakily.
And before you know it you are humming,
To that catchy little one, two, three, four.
With a five, six, seven, and eight nine-ing
At ten in a flash and now wanting more.
Only fourteen lines here for you to hum
Count it out with a bum, bum, bum, bum, bum.

## In The Stacks

### By: Kody Christiansen

Down below the ground I sit,
with the ancients and the new alike.
If it were darker and not electric lit,
deep inside I might catch an awful fright.
Who is there? A quiet voice asks.
And then I turn my head.
Calm like whisky in unopened casks,
quiet again, no sound, eerily like the dead.
I go back to my writing
about freedoms and mornings.
I write about a big circus - how exciting -
and then the great tent's adornings.
I read about a man named Nick,
and his job deep beneath the ground.
Dark for him, too, with his candlestick.
Pen to paper and then there is that sound.
My boy, my dear sweet boy,
are you sitting and dreaming things up?
No need to be coy,
in here knowledge overfloweth thine cup.
Just peek into my chest,
the pages are the oxygen I breathe.
I promise you the best,
my blood of text is everything you need.
With that last remark,

I decided it best to leave.
But she did create a spark.
This poem - created from her seed.
In the stacks and far below the ground.
You'll find your inspiration -
and may even hear the sound.
To those who journey under,
best of luck to you my friend.
I can say no more...
for this story has reached its end.

# Blinded by the Right

## By: Kody Christiansen

"It was all a fraud" - they screamed.
"The votes counted ... you must have dreamed."
For their powerful leader could never fall,
To them - the man - must have won it all.
Once so open-minded and a dear friend,
One-way paths led her to a dead end.
"Please," I beg, "Come back to the truth."
Then she points to the sky just like Babe Ruth.
"A gift from God is this Qualified Angel,
To release the country from a choking strangle.
You just can't see what he's done for me -
You just can't see his vision for our country."
I shake my head and snap my fingers in her face,
"Come back, come back, away from that place."
And for a brief moment, it was like my friend had
returned.
She opened her eyes and felt how they burned.
"Where am I? What happened? How can this be?
What did I do? And what did they do to me?"
"Listen, girl, you only have five minutes of clarity -
And what they did to you is not quite a rarity.
You're clouded, distracted, and blinded by the right.
The big lies they fed you - made you lose your sight.
But, all is not lost - please take this opportunity...

Drop the red glasses and come back to reality."
"Their VOICES are so loud and it's all that I hear,
Left or Right - the truth has become so unclear.
Democrat - Republican - those are just words.
To the other, each lives in a world of absurds.
Oh no! My eyes are getting cloudy again…
Raise your flag, this battle is not just pretend."
MAGA, AOC, RBG … are acronyms of this war -
So how do we find peace through an un-opening
door?
"I feel your passion but it is misguided by the right -
"Let me help," I say, "Help you find the light."
Lies on top of lies and a mountain in between -
Lies on top of lies - bound by the *huuuge* machine.
The truth, the truth - the truth will always be.
The truth, the truth - **the truth shall set us free.**

## The First Time.

### By: Kody Christiansen

I remember the day so clearly...
The first time that you were near me.
I was nervous and a little bit scared.
I was anxious and a bit unprepared.

The moment we touched was so fresh and so new.
I struggled at first - I knew not what to do.
But as the moment wore on it all became clear -
This is historic - and the best moment of the year.

In my hands, as I slid up and down your body,
I thought to myself, "Why does this feel so naughty?"
So wet, so smooth, so slippery... a mess -
Imagination ran wild with each touch and caress.

When finished with you - I left you to dry.
If you broke in time, I surely would cry.
Your porcelain figure - a creation of mine.
Born and fired from my very first time.

## When the bells call out to you.

### By: Kody Christiansen

BONG!
BONG!
BONG!
The
Sound
Of
The
Bells
High
Above
The Yard.
BONG!!!!
BONG!!!!
BONG!!!!
Ringing out each
Hour to alarm and
Scare the squirrels.
No, no. They ring to remind us
That time is ever-present and the
Day - it moves with the sun - now and
For eternity? Will it last? The bells that have
Rung from under the steeple for nearly 400 years
Will they last for 400 more? Will we last for that
long? Or is this familiar sound echoed against the red-
bricked Walls of this ancient University - but just a

whisper in the Song of time? Shh. Think twice and you'll miss it. A blip on The invisible radar that is the Creator of all that is seen and Unseen. Does this all-encompassing ear, our friend, hear the Bells as loud as we do? Each hour for us is, perhaps, a nano-Second for it. For him, for her, the Goddess or the God, the dark And the light, the everything and the nothing. Tick tock, tick tock But I do not hear the clock. Not the tower one or the inner one it Seems. Time - here in the Yard - is fleeting but it also feels like it Will never end. When the rain falls and the colors of the chairs are Dampened by the tears of the unknown, we sit upon the ever grand Steps of the library built on the memory of death - and we shelter our Thoughts and Selves and Others under the awning of limited knowledge. For even with the millions of books that lay within - the books who have heard Those same bells for their whole lifetime or but a mere fraction of their lifetime - do not hold the answers to everything. Do not let the glittering logos and promise Of *veritas* fool you. The *truth* is that no matter how many bells or how many books

One obtains

There

Is no

Answer.

When the bells

Call out to

You.

## Room 2 1 2

### By: Kody Christiansen

The elevator with its golden door smelled like piss.
Leading me to supposed salvation was
definitely a miss.
A needle on the floor someone had recently used.
My inner self cried out from being constantly abused.

"I did this to myself," was not something I thought.
The voice in the bottle was not something I fought.
Drink. Drink. Drink. The silencer - so loud.
Smoke. Smoke. Smoke. No reason to be proud.

Crushed crystals in snapped-off pipes.
Outside the shelter walls, I could not see lights.
No guidance, no love, no hope - all lost.
A multi-momentary high came at such a great cost.

Darkened rooms and a darkened spirit.
Peeling paint - I just had to get near it.
The white specks on the black door - so curious -
A message lay below, I scratched quick and so furious.

I scoffed as I scuffed and unveiled the note...
Words from above printed - not wrote.
"The Lord is your shade," it started out

"The Lord will keep you?" I almost did shout.

Where was this God that let me get here?
Where was this God that let me feel fear?

When the message was fully revealed at 2 1 2
I had a moment of clarity that came into view.
I could have been dead - many times near death
What does this mean? Is there a little hope left?

It would be nearly a year before I found my sobriety.
But it was then that the message was so clear to me.
The unexplainable, the universe, a being with no strife.
The light in my darkness - keeping watch over my life.

## BEEP ZAP BOOP ZOT

*An occasional poem that rhymes!*

By: Kody Christiansen

There once was a human named Grace.
She wrote poems all over the place.
Grace knew a gal named Lauren.
The poems she wrote weren't borin'
They both had a friend named Ryan
His poems had us laughin' and cryin'.
And Ryan had a friend named Bethany.
Poems so good - thought they'd be the death of me.
She had a pal named Braden.
His heartfelt poems were of quality makin'.
Then there was his pal named Helen.
Her mind-blowing poems had my mind meltin'.
Helen had a buddy named Juliana -
Whose outdoor poem was a stunna'.
Juliana made a buddy named Anthony:
Poems amazing - velvet voice - face mystery!
Anthony had an associate named Sabrina -
Words so quick you'd think they
were from Turner, Tina.
Sabrina's associate was named Nathanael -
And his great poems made me think, "Well dang, yall!"
Then there was a student named Ana.

I read her poems online and I am a fan - ah.
Can't forget her classmate named Kristen,
Who's poems I made sure I wasn't missin'.
And now we come to the writer named Kody,
You're reading his words now and he is me!
And this poem wouldn't be complete
on this occasion...
Without a mention of the person
who is the inspiration.
A big thanks to Professor Barber
who is sometimes a Robot.
A wonderful teacher - with the occasional
"beep zap boop zot!"
Now, back to the readings with all of our friends -
So sorry this poem and this class has to end.
Bye!

## Because I stopped for Death

### *Inspired by Emily Dickinson*

By: Kody Christiansen

Because I stopped for Death --
I saw something I shouldn't see --
A man I helped just days before --
Life-less was he.

I turned his body over  -
And when I saw his face
I knew that it was too late,
For he had left this place --

I felt a chill and sorrow down
my spine -- on the street --
Where people passed all around --
No shoes upon his feet --

His name -- we did not know --
And so I asked around --
"Mike," one person said --
"Is the man that's on the ground."

Before I could start the CPR --
The EMTs arrived --

They tried to do their very best,
But, it was clear the man had died.

No one should die -- like that
In front of a wealthy university --
I wanted to write a tribute --
For all the world to see --

This man was our neighbor --
He was a human being --
He deserved a life much better,
I hope, now, that is seen,

Because I stopped for Death --
I found life -- a complex story --
Gratitude and Anger --
For a man no one could see.

## Borrowed Voices

### By: Kody Christiansen

Up there on the pulpit, they speak -
This is the moment which many do seek -
"We have come together to make this happen!"
A sleight of hand - a pencil with a bubble filled in.

How many posters and flyers were made?
How many prayers did they ask to be prayed?
How many marched for their hopes
and their dreams?
How many times have they been ripped
from the seams?

Every single time - when the old clock stalls -
Intense frustration is sprayed all over the walls.
Do what you say - and say what you do...
All that we ask is your words to be true.

How many lies and promises not kept?
How did you sleep - last time that you slept?
How many moments were full of untruth?
How did you do it without any proof?

It's not just you - you unnamed politician -
It's all and above, our country's mortician.

Death by vote - ironic at best.
So many times they failed at the test.

How did it happen - this time and again?
How did the cycle not find its end?
How did these become our only choices?
How did they win with our borrowed voices?

## Remember before?

By: Kody Christiansen


Ah-choo! Loud and clear.
What a sneeze rang through the air!
Glances at her - scared.
Subliminal sound.
Fear and Distress all around.
Where did it come from?
Where does it go now?
Through the air - dancing - like, wow!
The doctor is in.
Thoughts of nightmares here.
Years of fright - away we steer
This is all of us.
Remember before?
Freely we walked out the door.
But not anymore.
The whole world did stop.
Life plans, like movies, did flop.
A sneeze changed the world.
The messages - clear.
In every language we hear.
Whispers tomorrow.
Do you hear us all?
We are done with this long fall.
Bring us back to life.

So loud - the silence
Broken dreams with indifference.
Wake us up again.
No Zoom - acting mime -
Off the screen and back in time.
Swing sweet chariot-
Low and fast come forth,
From the west, east, south, and north -
Now, let freedom ring!

## Something To End On.

Well, "that's all folks" ... the rabbit did say.
Through that black hole, then gone away.
Memories of easier days when my eyes were wide.
Time back then was definitely on my side.
As we grow up and some of us grow old,
We think back to the moments and
stories we were told.
A warm embrace by a mother no longer with us,
and a table around where life we did discuss.
The television has grown right alongside me.
Bigger and brighter with so much to see.
I wish you were here to watch us both.
I wish you were here to see the real growth.
The world it has grown, too.
It kept spinning without you.
But you never left my mind.
Your spirit, inside, I can find.
Mother, my best friend, I lost you too soon.
I think of you fondly when I look to the moon.
It has been so many years since you have been gone -
But your memory, today, gives me
something good to end on.

Love is Everlasting.

# Final Reflection and Debriefing:

## *Written in 2020*

Hard to believe it is time to write the final debriefing. The semester has seemed to go by so fast ... but also so slow concurrently. Isn't it strange how time works?

This course has allowed me to dive deeper into my love for poetry, discover new poets (right there in that Zoom room) who inspired me, and served as an outlet for emotions that came up when unexpected trauma fell into my proverbial lap.

I found that I definitely have a "go-to" style, but exploring outside of the style is also fun and rewarding. I will continue to write poetry when my feelings require - because I have found that it is one of the best, most cathartic, ways to get a little healing started. That recognition was amplified this semester. (PS. I added four lines to *Remember Before?* because I wanted to make the poem feel even bigger and more wide-reaching. Universal to the max!)

I look forward to one day taking the Advanced Poetry class with Professor Barber - and maybe it will be on campus! Fingers crossed for a return to semi-normal one day soon, so my poetry can move from sneezes impacting the world — back to lost loves and romance, ala Taylor Swift and Adele. (Two wonderfully resourceful poets.)

# Chapter 6

# Poems:
# Dying Well

*Original poems written by Kody Christiansen inspired by the Harvard course: "Dying Well" taught by Dr. Jason Silverstein and with teaching assistants Jacob Krueger and Blake Remington. 2022.*

Table of Contents:

1. Dying Well

2. Hope, Confidence, Desire

3. Why?

4. Letting Go.

5. Grieving.

6. Is Death Bad? (The Urn)

7. What Makes Life Good?

8. Sudden Death.

9. Eternal Life.

## Introductions

## (Dying Well)

Fall into thee with open hearts and open minds.
Be free in thought but careful with what one finds.
The journey we take together is a bit like life itself,
Ups and downs, round and rounds, and
unopened books upon the shelf.
Dare you reach a little deeper inside?
Uncover the truths and lies where they hide?
Tell yourself what you thought before -
or dream of something new,
Imaginations and relations will change
before this moment is through.
Take down that book, dust it off, and open it real wide.
Let the waves of emotions wash over and
take you in with the tide.
Not just a class on death but a
plan of action in lessons.
Every chapter, every speaker,
will leave their lasting impressions.
Introductions are made and we watch
the stories unfold -
A safe space for memories and beloved
narratives retold.

# Hope, Confidence, Desire

**Hope:**
Sparks of joy in a little child's eyes,
A mother looks up with her happy sighs.
Each day is a gift they choose to enjoy.
Sparks of hope they decide to employ.

**Confidence:**
Another day has gone by and the sun it did set.
Minutes and hours are spent without a hint of regret.
Confidence in the words they have
been assuredly given -
He will still be here, they know,
when the sun has re-risen.

**Desire:**
A desire to live a life with him forever.
A desire to live a life with her together.
Inside the intruder has different plans
A desire to draw a line in the sands

**Ending:**
No matter the hope, the confidence, and desire -
It will all end when it is time to eternally retire.

# Why?

Why should I even try to fight this?
Wouldn't my attempt just be amiss?

Why would I put myself through that pain?
What if I never saw you again?

Why do the words not calm me like before?
Could they be hiding what is really at the core?

Why does death need to be this thing so mysterious?
Can't I just be mad, live my life in minutes so furious?

Why does the timeline not match
what's in *my* mind?
Days move fast but where is the slow
solace I *must* find?

Why are there so many questions about
death never spoken?
Doesn't our life, our love, deserve peace
before being broken?

Why does it come down to a tearful goodbye?
Why can't it just last forever? I die.

## Letting Go.

Sitting there in the room is the Death Ambassador.
Quietly waiting nearby with a message inside of her.

Close to suffering and walking into the pain -
Tomorrow will be there and a lot more of the same.

Not something found present in a regular blood test,
A palpable sense of loss, despair, and grief's loneliness.

The Ambassador of Death is trained
to detect these fluctuations,
To bring a voice of peace in
these toughest of situations.

But where do they go when they need to be heard?
Where do they mend their hearts with
an embrace and warm word?

The Death Ambassador does not put on a show -
It is their calling to help people let go.

To find quiet and gratitude
in the last moments on earth,
Sitting there in the room
confirming a lived life full of worth.

## Grieving

"A mental, physical, or social reaction"
is how they try to describe it.
Feelings so loud that those words
they don't quite quiet.
"A normal reaction," they say,
"when one encounters real loss."
Clinical terminology so quick
out the window we do toss.

Everyone experiences grief differently, you see,
How you respond is unlike the response
one will see from me.

A tear that falls - retreating away from society –
A drink thrown back, careful now, take away his key.
A new hobby one never could have expected,
Or a spiritual awakening lost but now resurrected.

How long is one allowed to be in bereavement?
Is shorter better ... a detached emotional achievement?
Whatever you can do to give your heart a little relief -
Let no one tell you how to heal and live
within your grief.

## Is Death Bad?

## (The Urn)

Is death bad? I guess, it is how you see it.
Some say it could be - but one cannot commit.

If the life to be lived thereafter
was destined to be painful,
Would one stick around if
life would not be gainful?

What if a sealed letter appeared at your door -
It held your death date, a fact you knew not before.

Would you open that letter or
choose to take your chance?
Make a deal with the Devil or
with the fates a little dance?

"So much opportunity ahead of her,"
the pastor he would say.
But how do we really know that her
life would have gone that way?

The fact is that we cannot know -
no one has ever made it back -
From that great beyond to explain -

when our minds go black.

"Live life to the fullest," -
the often overused saying we hear.
But, really, "hold them close"
is the one to hold dear.

Message in a bottle - flown to outer space.
Memories of good times - locked inside this vase.

## What Makes Life Good?

The simple things, the little things,
and the love-filled things
Are the moments and enjoyments
that life ultimately brings.
Singing songs that history sang and
reprising dances from another time,
A repeating cycle of sensations that
are threaded from yours to mine.
A willowed web of lust and love –
of simplicity and complexness,
What makes life good, of course,
is the lack of understandness.
Fear not for things out of your control
for they can never hurt you.
Go forth, hold tight, be strong, and love –
before your time is through.
What makes life good is not a plan or a rigid structure -
It is the time we have right now
and the hope for a brighter future.
Hope is the key. Optimism is the door.
Love is on the other side.
Be wise with these three things -
what makes life good is on the inside.

## Sudden Death.

Fall fast, sweet angels, your time to go has come -
Unheard of choices made -
at the place that you fell from.
What were the options while waiting up in there?
Fall free, with choice, or go later,
breathless without air?
No one could have seen this coming;
a tragedy so unthinkable -
Your memory, your life... a choice -
to some unbelievable.

There is no person living that dare to judge you now,
For in that moment what would we do
if time did not allow?

A minute, a few seconds, a flight to another world -
Sadness dark and dreary, as so many lives unfurled.
It was not sudden death for you -
but the only way one could foresee,
With grace you fell and in an instant
then you ceased to be.
But what goes down must come up,
your caged spirit flew.
That date in September - I promise,
we will never forget you.

## Eternal Life.

On his deathbed, today, he reaches for the buzzer -
A nurse, she comes real quick,
and he motions for her.

"I want to be surrounded closely...
by the ones I truly love."
"I need to know that something...
is waiting for me above."

The nurse, she calls the family,
and the hospital chaplain -
Enveloped by their presence,
he sees a welcome sign: "*the end.*"

His body stays on earth,
the family makes arrangements -
His soul floating in the ether
is making new agreements.

What if the soul leaves the body
and breaks into a million pieces?
To only come together with others -
making a new existence.

Eternal life may not be currently
available on this planet  -

But, perhaps, someday,
our scientists will find a way to do it.


And until then, we live each day
with hope for the great unknown -
And at the end, it is about good things,
and proof that we have grown.

## Processing with Poetry : A Companion Piece

Death is one of the common connections that all humans can relate to, because, no matter how hard we might try, we are all going to die. Our bodies fall apart, they break down, sometimes our mind goes before our body, sometimes we last well into old age, and sometimes we are taken suddenly without any time to prepare. Once it happens, we get cremated, we get buried, we get stuffed in a mausoleum, or placed inside a green pod attached to a sapling that then is planted and, in a way, gives us a new life. The *we* that we knew ceases to exist – but what we leave behind, is often a deep tear in the fabric of the lives of those who loved us. We will never know how our loved ones or our dear friends ultimately dealt with our passing, but history shows us there are many ways in which people go through bereavement.

Dr. Sue Morris, from Dana-Farber Cancer Institute, performed a study in 2017 of family members going through bereavement and asked questions about how the hospital's bereavement team was successful in the ways they helped the families or where they could use improvement. Out of the 140 participants, only 24 answered the question that asked what the team could have done differently; the most common response was that there was, " . . . a lack of contact or contact that was impersonal after the death." People want to be seen and heard, they long for connection, and when they are grieving, an impersonal message might drive them deeper into their grief even if momentarily. If only 24 out of 140 people answered that question, that must mean that for the majority of instances, the team was helpful in preparing and consoling their clients. Of the many ways to deal with grief suggested by bereavement teams and in palliative care, there is one that seems to be often overlooked or underutilized; poetry.

Poetry has been used by humans in bereavement for centuries and has produced some of the most famous poetic works of all time. Emily Dickinson's "Because I could not stop for Death" speaks grief through lyrics when she wrote in the first stanza, "Because I could not stop for Death – / He kindly stopped for me – / The Carriage held but just Ourselves – / And Immortality." Death, she says, does not wait for anyone – it comes when it is time. Nasrullah Mambrol points to the 1847 death of Emily's close friend, Olivia Coleman, as the inspiration for this renowned poem by stating in an article that the woman was, "the beautiful older sister of Emily's close friend Eliza M. Coleman, who died of a tubercular hemorrhage while out riding in a carriage." Emily does not specifically state a name but, perhaps, that is not necessary for bereavement poetry; the author knows who it is for and the people she shared it with did, too.

Another famous poem titled *O Captain! My Captain!* written in 1865, is a message of grief written during bereavement and is Walt Whitman's elegy to the slain President Lincoln. Whitman who had never met Lincoln face to face, felt such a strong connection with him that after hearing of his death wrote this poem during his own mourning period to process his grief. Almost with disbelief, at the end of the first stanza, Whitman writes, "But O heart! heart! Heart! / O the bleeding drops of red, / Where on the deck my Captain lies, / Fallen cold and dead." The question is asked sometimes whether we can grieve or be in bereavement for someone we never really knew in person – a celebrity, a monarch, or a President. Clearly, the answer is yes. Whitman pours his heart into this poem for a man he never met, but a man who everyone felt like they knew and, as we know from history, a man who inspired so many. More modern-day examples of this type of complicated grief would be instances such as the death of Princess Diana or tragically losing celebrities like Selena or Tupac to gun violence, and even more recently the matured-age deaths of Betty White and Her Majesty Queen Elizabeth II. Many people around the world mourned for these famous faces without ever meeting them in person – and, one can assuredly assume, that there were many songs, books, and poems written in grief about their deaths. Writing poetry is a pure form of expression and can help people cope when other outlets may not work for them.

Poetry lasts forever for some authors - a legacy that is everlasting. Many poets have pondered about eternity and, perhaps, these works can give us clues. Can poetry answer the questions about the end? People who write about death, or even those who may write on their deathbeds, may hold the answer to what comes next – or they can at least inspire our imaginations and hopes. Mambrol ponders what Dickinson was saying in her poem on death and wrote, "At one end of the spectrum are those who view the poem as Dickinson's ultimate statement of the soul's continuance; at the other end are those who see the poem as intrinsically ironic and riddled with doubt about the existence of an afterlife; in the middle are those who find the poem indisputably ambiguous." Is that not what it is all about; poetry, art, life, and death – a journey of ambiguousness, ironies, love, and the questions that can never be answered? If poems are the thing that helps someone process, then hand them a pen or a laptop and let the healing begin.

# Bibliography

Dickinson, Emily. "Because I Could Not Stop for Death – (479) by…" Poetry Foundation. Poetry Foundation. Accessed December 12, 2022. https://www.poetryfoundation.org/poems/47652/because-i-could-not-stop-for-death-479.

Davies, Elizabeth A. "Why we Need More Poetry in Palliative Care." *BMJ Supportive & Palliative Care* 8, no. 3 (09, 2018): 266. doi:https://doi.org/10.1136/bmjspcare-2017-001477.        http://search.proquest.com.ezp-prod1.hul.harvard.edu/scholarly-journals/why-we-need-more-poetry-palliative-care/docview/2307156725/se-2.

Kilgore, Georgette. "Tree Pod Burial: How It Works in 2022 (Costs, Locations, & More)." 8 Billion Trees: Carbon Offset Projects & Ecological Footprint Calculators, September 21, 2022. https://8billiontrees.com/eco-friendly-natural-products/tree-pod-burial/.

Mambrol, Nasrullah. "Analysis of Emily Dickinson's Because I Could Not Stop for Death." Literary Theory and Criticism. Literariness.org, July 5, 2020. https://literariness.org/2020/07/05/analysis-of-emily-dickinsons-because-i-could-not-stop-for-death/#:~:text=Schol-ars%20have%20suggested%20that%20Dickin-son's,out%20riding%20in%20a%20carriage.

Morris, Sue, Block, Susan. Lessons from bereaved families: Insights about how the care of patients impacts bereavement. J Clin Oncol. 2017;35(31):87. doi:10.1200/JCO.2017.35.31_suppl.87.

Whitman, Walt. "O Captain! My Captain! by Walt Whitman." Poetry Foundation. Poetry Foundation. Accessed December 12, 2022. https://www.poetryfoundation.org/poems/45474/o-captain-my-captain.

Original poems written by Kody Christiansen inspired by the Harvard course: "Dying Well" taught by Dr. Jason Silverstein and with teaching assistants Jacob Krueger and Blake Remington.

# Chapter 7

# Poems: Personal Projects in the Elsewhere

These poems are a collection of works written outside the classroom while in my time at NYU, Harvard, Cambridge, and elsewhere ... the New Yorks, Moroccos, and Hollywoods of it all. Creativity Ungraded.

Table of Contents:

## The Little Cowboy

Blue eyes covered by a perfectly steamed hat.
It takes precision to make it fit just like that.
Brown leather boots too big for him too.
But that is just what them little cowboys do.
You can smell it all before you even hear the sounds.
For in the stockyards the steers
are a makin' their rounds.
Yeehaw and woohoo are a ritualist call
All before the bronco bucks and causes a fall.
A little baby goat and a sheep we did pet
In a little zoo where them boots did get wet
"Don't cry little cowboy
'cause that's not what men do."
Words from a father before he knew what I knew.
Back then I didn't see rainbows
through my Texanly eyes.
But years later the world produced one
from those darkened skies.

# In Memory of My Dear Student Government

With faded dreams and crushed optimism, I wrote.
The voice of the people in an emotion-filled note.
How dare they speak of us as less than we are.
When we strived for our rights and got very far.
Experience and age did not prepare me for this -
To battle with advisors and being so hit and miss.
Was there ever a moment when I felt respected?
Or was it all a dream? Because none was detected.
I knew we deserved better than someone like you.
That's why we scream out for someone brand new.
Like as an apple sitting out too long at the store
Or just as you are - someone rotten to the core.
More students will come
and be faced with the same
As if you intend to keep playing
a never-ending game.
"Farwell to you," is something I wish I could say -
But for the people, I am determined to stay.
Meantime we rally, we fight, and we stand -
Thou, my friend, now you see the line in the sand.

## Still.

Between two worlds is where I live.
Am I her, or am I him?

The character becomes me now,
Or is it the truth that lies beneath my brow?

If I play this part for far too long,
Will the inner me be forever gone?

Or is this facade more of who I truly am?
When I remove this mask, will he still give a damn?

Does this man I love so dearly
See past the bluff and into my soul so clearly?

But when the truth is put on the table,
Will he speak words so sweet like a fable?

"Marry me, Be Mine... Just Stay."
A dream, a hope, of words I wish he would say.

If I am just me at the end of the day...
Will he still love me when I tell him
I am not what I play?

*( 2019 | Inspired by Shakespeare's Twelfth Night*
*- and my own personal life, obvi. )*

## Mi amor - no more.

My dearest boy - my man - *mi amor,*
How could you leave and walk out the door?

*La puerta de mi corazon* - slammed so tightly shut -
Broken inside - *tan roto* - no walls remain afront.

Friends, *amigos,* pals
while in your world of the bankers,
but in the dark - our *intimo* - I was so *brillante tu luz.*

I felt so alive the day you spoke a sweet, "*te amo.*"
But *muerto* inside the day you breathed, "I must go."

You taught me some *espanol* but more about love
But, now, *volar liberamente*
my handsome spanish dove.

If you love someone, delojas ir - they say.
*Espero queue vuelva a mi* - I pray.

## Wooden Planks and Little Frogs

Wooden planks and one little frog,
Meeting you did lift my dark fog.

The bonfire it raged in the clear moonlight,
These feelings for you I just couldn't fight.

Is he looking at me? Does he want more?
Why must his eyes open this door?

So shut off and contained
was my still beating heart.
But this guy and his brain
had me right from the start.

In the grassy field and in the sky when he flew,
His smile said the words and I knew that he knew.

In the daylight out there in the company of deer,
Our hands touched softly and I let go of my fear.

Open up to him I said and don't be afraid,
There's no way this one could lead you astray.

But looks can be deceiving
You can't always go believing

That a first date filled with magic,
Could turn into a week so tragic.

I can't totally blame him
for what happened to my heart.
I gave so much too quickly
and it all fell apart.

Maybe he was scared
from the newness of it all.
Or maybe he's afraid
to let down the steel veil of his wall.

I held his hand across the table
and his gaze in my eyes.
Why must those beautiful feelings
be the first thing that dies?

Seeing him now and just trying to be friends.
It doesn't really make a means to the ends.

STOP. I say to myself on those sporadic days.
You're a PRIZE my friend and you can't give it away.

I wanted to freeze time in the field by the logs,
Go back to the moment with you, me, and the frogs.

## My Memory Becomes a Wilderness of Elsewheres

Yesterday, I watched a film –
all scenes I don't remember -
Flickering past and future shots,
a bleak ending to November.

I see his face in my mind
from beyond the silvery screen.
Longing thoughts of him persist –
please stop and intervene.

Sorrowfully, I play a tune –
dreamt up inside my head,
No instrument can play this song –
if love is surely dead.

I float into an endless abyss
of whats and ifs and could ...
But I never stop to ask myself –
if I really should.

Have I not been hurt before?
This game so mad and free.
Who do the players play –
and who gets hurt but only me?

This act - in life - like the script
that writes itself unfolding,
Claims its stake in my heart,
his hand forever holding.

Penetrating deep inside,
the blood courses to my brain –
I only wish to remember him
and this bloody, beautiful pain.

The grass - so tall -
no one can hear or see my screams,
Wintery breath escapes like fog,
barely breaching atop the reeds.

Visions creep outside, then in –
timeless – wishing to grow stronger.
Come back to me –
my memories – and stay a little longer.

Elsewhere, he and I belong,
unbounded, a love without suppress.
Elsewhere, he and I are free,
lost in my shattered wilderness.

© 2023 | Kody Christiansen

# MAGAZINES

Photography and Paintings

# Magazines

The moment I met my idol. Heat Magazine, UK

# Chapter 8

# Ten Years, Eleven Photos

From 2013 - 2023

*Photos from Facebook Memories*

A couch on the street inspired this photo. In 2013, I was living in a nice apartment between Sunset Blvd and Santa Monica Blvd. I had a great job (that I didn't give my all to) and a nightlife (that soon took over). At the time, I thought this couch out on the street was perplexing. Just months later, I would be out on the street. West Hollywood - 2013

While in the first homeless shelter in NYC, I found out my Grandma Ellen passed away. My heartbreaking handling of the situation is chronicled in my first memoir. I did this chalk art outside the shelter to honor her. NYC - 2014

My backpack hangs on the door of my very own New York apartment. After nearly two years in the shelter system, I found an organization that helped me get this apartment. I was in my first month of sobriety. This apartment changed my life. The Bronx - 2015

2016 was a year of growth and dreams made real. I published my first memoir in May and, in June, celebrated one year of sobriety. The official book release party was held at Stonewall Inn. The book signings that followed allowed me to travel back to LA and Texas for the first time since leaving both cities. This year was a complete rebirth for me. NYC - 2016

My birthday cake. My second book. My bicoastal living. This year brought more dreams to life than I could have ever imagined. From speaking roles on television to additional book awards. I finally understood what I was capable of. And then, I did it. West Hollywood - 2017

NYU!! This year, I was accepted to the college I had been dreaming of going to since I was a teen. I also flew to Atlanta to film a scene in a Lifetime movie. I was doing acting work in both NYC and Hollywood. And my family of friends grew exponentially. Year three of sobriety and doors continued to open. NYC - 2018

At NYU, I pushed myself to maintain all As while exploring everything university life had to offer. I went to NYU London for my first summer abroad. No matter where I went in the world, the Universe always seemed to remind me of where I came from. This deli in Camden Town was one of those signs. London - 2019

One of my proudest moments in life up to this point came at a time when the whole world was at a standstill due to the pandemic. I graduated from NYU in an online ceremony in 2020, but the diploma on the wall made it real. I transferred to Harvard this year and a new world opened up for me. NYC - 2020

As the world started to open back up, I started to explore more of Harvard and academia. I spent a lot of time in Salem, MA. I also went to UCL in London for summer school and did a weekend class at Cambridge University. New dreams were activated. Salem - 2021

I was involved with so many amazing organizations at Harvard in 2022 and stood by my fellow students as we fought for things like meal plans, global peace, and our unhoused Harvard Square neighbors. Stress was at an all-time high, but ceramics became my cherished outlet. Harvard Ceramics - Cambridge, MA - 2022

Graduation at Harvard was incredible. I was asked to host the University LGBTQ+ graduation event, and two of my chosen family came to see me walk the stage. Summer created new bonds at GSAS, and a few months later, I was at Cambridge University, beginning my Master's Degree. Cambridge, MA - 2023

# Chapter 9

# Photography

**Class Assignments: NYU and Harvard**

NYU Photography - "Remnants" - 2019

NYU Photography - "Remnants" - 2019

NYU Photography - "Remnants" - 2019

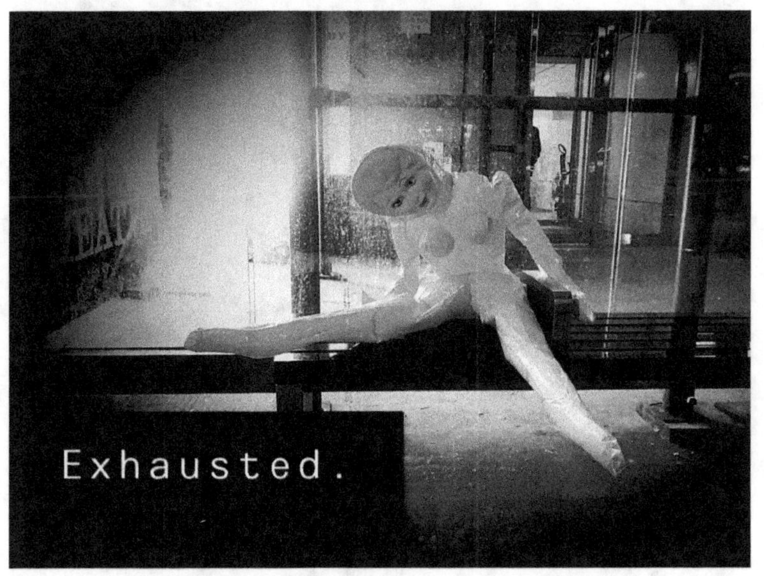


NYU Photography - "Remnants" - 2019

Morocco - "Cats in Rabat" - 2019

London - "The Fountain" - 2019

The Bronx - "Closed City" - 2020

The Bronx - "NYU 'Graduation'" - 2020

Harvard - "Guitar Bear Grinds" - 2021

Harvard - "Pet Rocks" - 2022

Cambridge University - "My New Home" - 2023

# Chapter 10

# Paintings

Class Assignments and Personal Projects

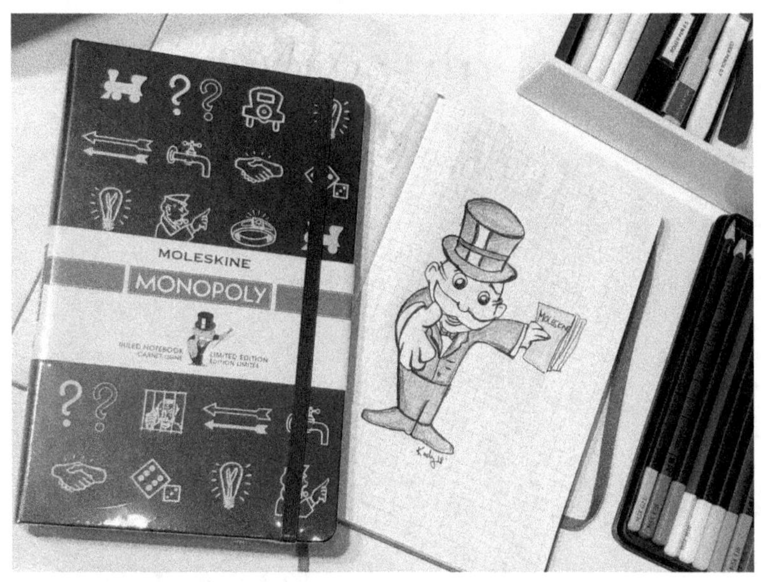


Drawn While Working - Moleskin NYC - 2018

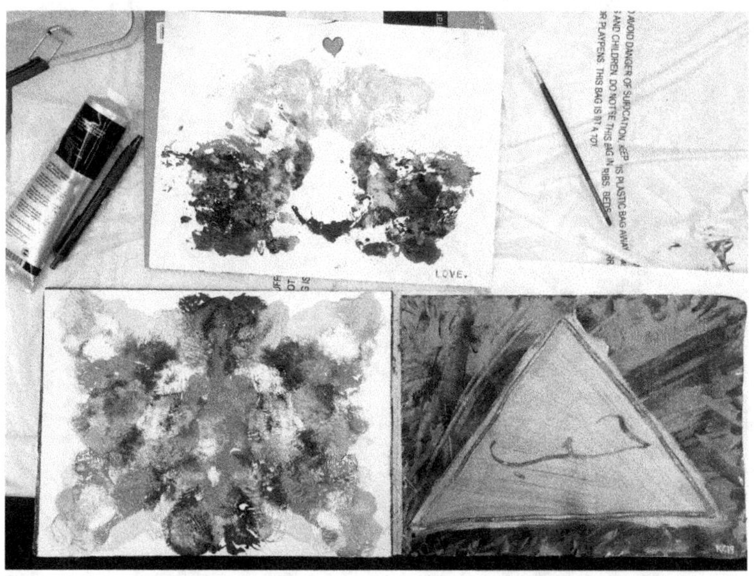

Professor Diane Leon's Painting Class - NYU - 2019

Personal Project - NYC - 2019

Perspective Practice - NYU - 2019

Personal Sketch - NYC - 2019

Harvard "Letters to a Young Artist" Course - Cambridge, MA - 2021

Harvard "Letters to a Young Artist" Course - Cambridge, MA - 2021

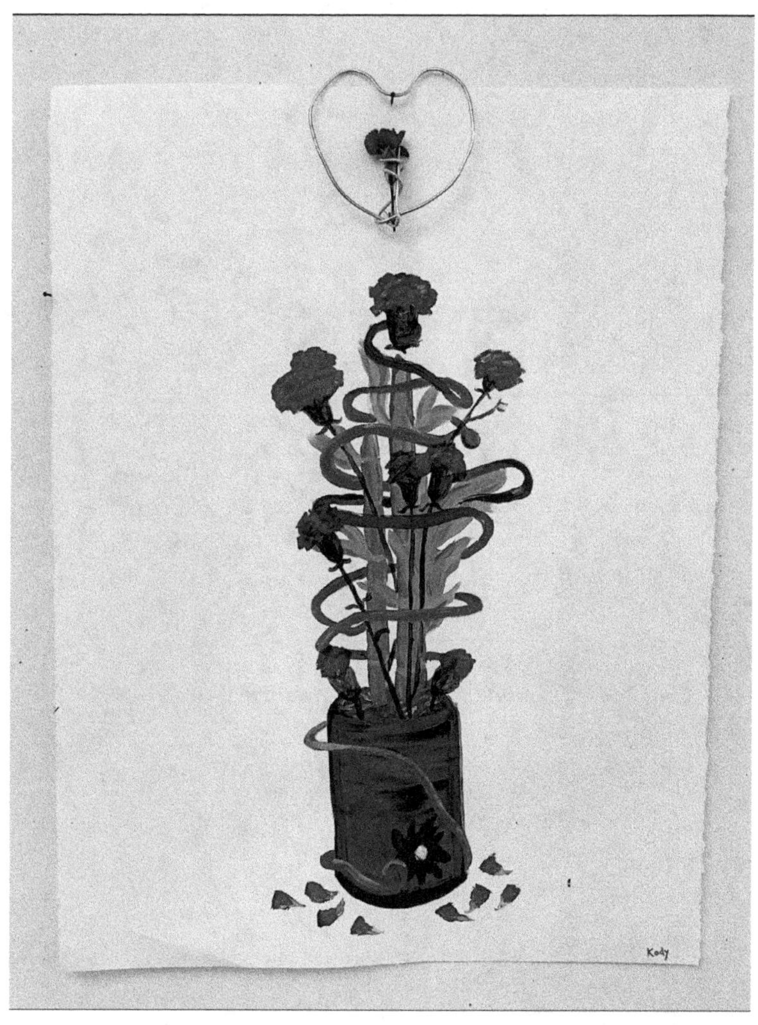

Harvard "Letters to a Young Artist" Course - Cambridge, MA - 2021

Harvard Ceramics Course - Cambridge, MA - 2022

Harvard "Quilting Circles: Painting" Course - Cambridge, MA - 2023

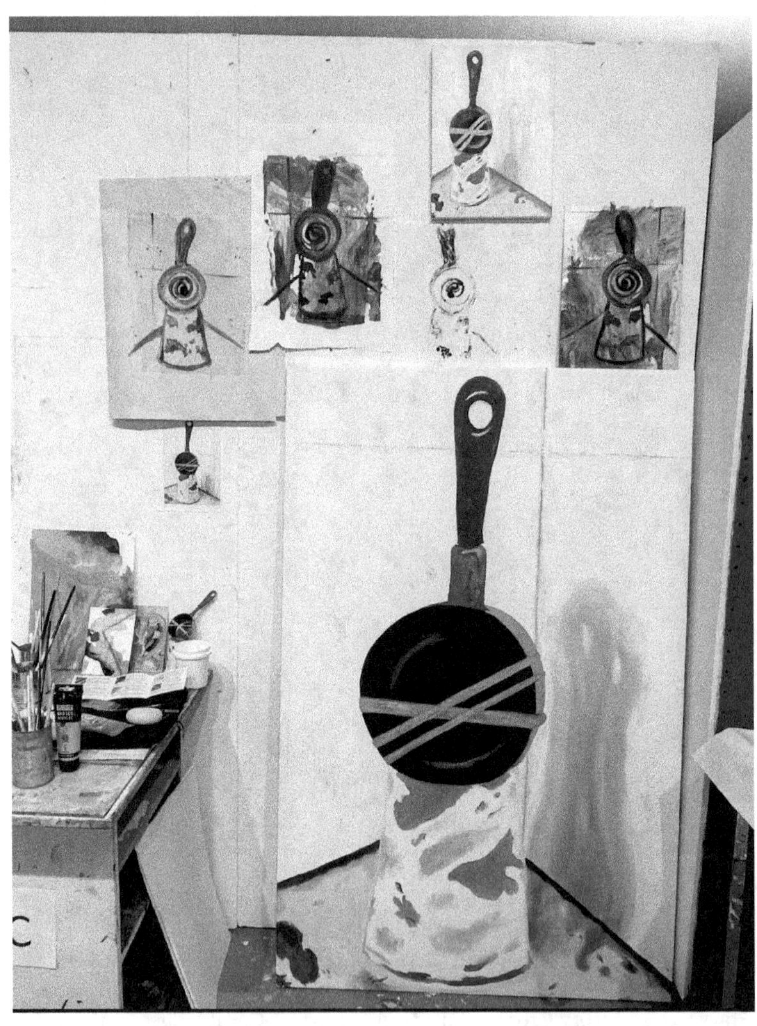

Harvard "Quilting Circles: Painting" Course - Cambridge, MA - 2023

Harvard "Quilting Circles: Painting" Course - Cambridge, MA - 2023

# Chapter 11

# Ten Years, Eleven Selfies

A Selfie Says a Thousand Words

2013 - West Hollywood - Before the Heartbreak.

2014 - New York City - Post-heartbreak, Pre-Dreams

2015 - New York City - Dreams Emerge

2016 - New York City - First Official (Selfie) Headshot

2017 - West Hollywood - I decided to grow a beard.

2018 - Atlanta - Filmed my first movie speaking role.

2019 - West Hollywood - Living bi-coastal, NYU, and doing Yoga.

2020 - New York City - FIVE years sober!!

2021 - Cambridge, MA - Harvard Undergraduate.

2022 - New York City - HER BODY, HER CHOICE.

2023 - Cambridge, UK - Cambridge University Master's Student

# POCKETBOOKS

Making Change: Academic Work

# Pocketbooks

Change.

Among so many things a pocketbook contains, one
    of them is always change.
But change is so hard to come by.
Not the pennies or pence that scatter the street or
    hidden in the cushion, but *real* change.

"He'll never change."
"He doesn't want to change."
"Change just isn't possible for someone like that."

Well, I call bullshit.

To be fair, though, I believed that for so long.
That I was incapable of change.
That some people in my life could
never change either.
But change was possible for me.
Change is possible for all of us.
We just have to want it. Seek it. Save it.
Then all things become possible.

So make a change. Inspire change.
Write it. Draw it. Sing it. Act it. Do it.

# Chapter 12

# A Universal Love: The Un-Queering of Brokeback Mountain

By
Kody Christiansen
Harvard | ALB | 2023

Submitted for:
*The Art of Film* | Harvard University AFVS Course

## A Universal Love:
## The Un-Queering of *Brokeback Mountain*

Gay cowboys and a "gay western."[1] Well, if those are the often-used two-word descriptions of a film, would that not immediately make it a queer film? The obvious answer is yes, but Brokeback Mountain is not as gay as it sounds. The film is, first and foremost, in the eyes of its director, Ang Lee, "...a love story." In fact, Lee did not even want it to be called "...a gay film."[2] But, when the two male main characters are struggling with their sexuality and ultimately fall in love – and consummate said love – is it not fair, then, to call it a queer film? Why stray away from that word or similar nomenclature? Mainstream success and Middle American expectations are why, of course. So, how does one un-queer a movie that centers around a queer love story? It takes a team of cinematic and marketing masters to pull off the task of un-queering a tale of gay cowboy love – and in Brokeback Mountain, it is done through meticulously crafted shots that evoke anticipation, attractive actors chosen to appeal to specific demographics, the power of the gaze, the subtleties of gendering in the relationship between the two male protagonists, and strategic interviews and advertisements that expertly steer the narrative consumers digest long before they ever enter the theater.

Intriguingly, Brokeback Mountain begins as a subversion of expectations, beckoning audiences with the promise of a groundbreaking exploration of queer love in an unlikely setting – the rugged, traditional American West. Yet, it cleverly navigates the tightrope between challenging norms and catering to a broader audience, all while maintaining the integrity of its central love story. It's a cinematic dance, a Texas two-step between art and commerce, where every frame, every look, every word, and every choice on and off-screen is orchestrated to entice and engage without alienating the Middle America viewers who might be apprehensive about venturing into unfamiliar territory.

### The Trail to Un-Queering

Like a seasoned sheepherder navigating a well-worn trail, this paper will follow the path set forth by the five key aspects introduced in the opening: shots, actors, gendering, the gaze, and marketing. Much like the determined herder ensuring the safety of their flock, this exploration will guide you through the intricate details of how these elements were harnessed to transform "Brokeback Mountain" into a film that resonated with a broad audience while still preserving the essence of its groundbreaking love story. Additionally, this paper will offer a concise movie summary, allowing readers to reacquaint themselves with the cinematic masterpiece that is now over fifteen years old.

In our journey through the cinematic wilderness,

we will make frequent stops at pivotal in-film scenes, using them as reference points to illuminate the film's nuanced strategies. Moreover, this expedition will be strengthened by the insights and wisdom of scholars, critics, and writers who have dissected "Brokeback Mountain" over the past nearly two decades since its release. These scholarly works include but are not limited to, essays such as "I Ain't Queer: Love, Masculinity, and History in Brokeback Mountain" by Leigh Boucher and Sarah Pinto, "Why I Hate That I Loved Brokeback Mountain" by Dwight A. McBride, "Queer Persona and the Gay Gaze in Brokeback Mountain: Story and Film" by Clifton Snider, and Laura Mulvey's seminal "Visual Pleasure and Narrative Cinema."

So, fasten your seatbelt and saddle up for an exhilarating linguistic journey as we embark on an in-depth investigation into how the filmmakers masterfully executed the un-queering of "Brokeback Mountain."

### Summary and Sunsets

While there is no happy ending to this film, there are a few beautiful sunset moments in the wide-open gorgeousness of nature and an immense love that is felt by both the two main characters on screen and the attentive viewing audience of the iconic movie. The film begins in Wyoming with two good-looking and straight-acting cowboys, Ennis Del Mar (Heath Ledger) and Jack Twist (Jake Gyllenhaal), who both take a job herding sheep together for a season up on a mountain called Brokeback. In the span of a few movie months, the two men form an unmistakable bond of passion that is driven by lust and eventually develops into a seriously unshakeable connection that teeters on the line of love. Over the next twenty (film) years, the two meet up for "fishing trips" where no fishing occurs; rather, they experience stolen moments together outside of their day-to-day closeted lives. Through those romantic meetups, their love solidifies into something both men wish they didn't have to live without. But Ennis has a wife and two daughters, and Jack and his wife have a son – and even though Jack constantly asks Ennis to run away and start a life with him, they both remain closeted for the remainder of their relationship. Their story ends in tragedy the day Ennis receives a returned postcard with the word "DECEASED" stamped in red across his own hand-writing.[3] Jack was beaten to death in a gay-bashing in a random Texas field, and Ennis is compelled to find closure. Their love story ends with Ennis making the trip to the house belonging to Jack's parents, and a hidden message of love in Jack's closet is discovered when Ennis finds both of their shirts they wore on Brokeback Mountain together on one hanger, sleeve in sleeve, like an eternal embrace. The film ends with a shot of Ennis' closet in his Wyoming trailer home, where the shirts are now hanging next to a postcard of Brokeback Mountain.

*Shooting the Shots*

Ahh, love. An awards-season-sweeping and main-stream-ground-breaking love story deserves a back-drop like no other, naturally, and director Ang Lee did not disappoint in this regard. Up on the moun-tain, deep in the valleys, and high on the hills of the fictional Brokeback Mountain, the sky, the trees, the rocks, and the grass are all players in the story right alongside our handsome main characters. The less sprawling backdrops, the more average buildings, and the locations that make up the film actually help create the un-queering effect and form the unspoken clues in the minds of the viewer that this is not a "gay film" but a Western love story where the two people falling in love happen to both be men. Filmed in dif-ferent parts of Canada, the home and work life aspects of the Wyoming and Texas backdrops are created by using real places about 100 miles south of Calgary in towns named Cowley and Rockyford, respectively.[4]

In the opening scene, we are told that this is the rough and tumble West and the filmmakers make sure the viewers know it when a literal tumbleweed blows by in the background behind the foreman's car as he speeds into his trailer office. This is not a glamorous office in a big city; it is a trailer in the middle of nowhere, where only manly men would go to look for a job. That's what the director wanted the view-ers to think, but there are clues from the beginning that these two manly men are destined for something more.

A few moments before the tumbleweed scene, there is a medium shot of Ennis leaning up against the trailer with his hat covering his eyes in that idyllic cowboy pose, which is then cut to a wide shot of Jack getting out of his sputtering truck in a huff because it is not running properly. Ennis slowly lifts his head and glances at Jack, then Jack glances back in a close-up shot – and the camera catches the slightest bit of a smirk before it cuts from Jack; he feels the energy. This moment, though, is not scandalous, sultry, or even seductive; it isn't even coded as a queer moment unless you look closely for that tell-all smirk. All these moments could have been more salacious or more de-finitively queer if, say, the camera had lingered longer on Jack or Ennis had not looked away so quickly. There is the first hint of gay shame both men feel in that encounter and Leo Bersanti explains this type of moment in *Is the Rectum a Grave?* where he says, "In shame . . . the eyes turn away from the object and are, so to speak, directed back at the subject's own face: full of ambivalence, he looks at himself being looked at."[5] The moment they first met could have read more queer if they had locked eyes – but they didn't – and in that initial moment, the way the actors played it, the way the director constructed it, and the way the camera caught it, all set the tone for the rest of the film's overarching theme that this is "not a gay film" but a "love story."[6]

## *Roping in the Right Actors*

For a love story about two closeted homosexual cowboys to be visually consumed by a wider audience (aka the mainstream moviegoers from middle America) and branch outwards far and wide, one must consider what visuals would be most well-received by the most people. In 2006, a year after Brokeback Mountain was released, the United States saw a slew of same-sex marriage bans passed in Alabama, Idaho, South Dakota, Tennessee, Virginia, Wisconsin, and Colorado. It seemed as if the "mainstream" wasn't exactly ready to see a love story about two gay cowboys in the early 2000s, so, how did Ang Lee and the team make this love story such a huge success both critically and commercially? Mr. Lee created a recipe for success: do not mention the word gay in the film and then hire two classically handsome, tall, one blonde and one brunette, with puppy dog eyes, chiseled abs and jawline, and biceps for days . . . and, of course, white and already budding stars in their respective careers. Clifton Snider points out the verbal un-queering of the film as he notes the lack of queer words in his article *Queer Persona and the Gay Gaze in Brokeback Mountain* when he states, "Ennis and Jack never use the words homosexual or gay to describe themselves and their relationship, nor, for that matter do they use the word, love." They never use the words gay or love, that is true, but the actors are very convincing without those words, which speaks to the filmmakers' keen eye when it came to finding the right people who would bring the characters to life on film.

Heath Ledger and Jake Gyllenhaal were the perfect casting for these roles because they appealed to so many people – the gay male viewers, of course, but also the heterosexual female audience who were more open to watching a film where two handsome, manly men roll around shirtless and kiss. Dwight A. McBride said that as an audience " . . . we have been prepared to receive a certain type of gay man [as a viewer]" and describes that man as "white, masculine, straight-acting, good-looking, and therefore sympathetic."

Perhaps McBride is right – it would be another ten years before the first gay film, *Moonlight*, featuring a black cast would win somewhat similar critical acclaim and commercial appeal. So, what if our main characters, our cornfed cowboy hunks, had been black in 2005? McBride thinks it wouldn't have worked at all and says, "Two African American men could not possibly have been viewed as representing universal gay male experience in the way that the whiteness of the characters of *Brokeback Mountain* can and does."[7] Thankfully, McBride's piece written in 2007 has not aged well in that respect, and movies like *Moonlight* and television shows like *Love, Victor* are proving that BIPOC gay films and shows can, in fact, tell the universal gay male experience and be successful with critics and viewers alike – without the need to un-queer any aspect of the productions to be more palpable to the mainstream.

### Gendering the Cowboy Couple

In the heterosexual world, there are men and women and each one usually takes on the traditional sexual role when in the bedroom. In the gay world, there are tops, bottoms, and men who are versatile when performing the act of sexual pleasure – that is how gay male coitus traditionally functions on average. Outside of the bedroom (or tent, in the case of Ennis and Jack), do those positions also determine one's role in the relationship? Clifton Snider seems to think both men do fit a particular gay persona and says, "If Ennis and Jack were born gay, that means they fit an archetypal gay persona."[8] So, if one gathers by the sexual positions assumed in the first sexual act the cowboys take part in, then Ennis is a top and Jack is a bottom. This is later confirmed on at least two separate occasions in the film: one when Ennis flips his wife over during sex with the lights off to imagine it is Jack, and towards the end of the film when Ennis calls Jack "one of those boys" who goes off to Mexico to get no-strings-attached pleasure by tops (Jack confirms this by saying it's something "I don't hardly never get," referring to being topped by Ennis).

If Ennis is a top and Jack is a bottom, which is not ever specifically said, how are mainstream audiences supposed to connect that to something in these two characters that they recognize within themselves? The filmmakers used their sexual positions, actions, and mannerisms to help *gender* the couple into a more understandable heteronormative association. Boucher and Pinto dive deeper into the gendered relationship by revealing, "Not only in their relationship with each other, but also in their relationship with the world (and camera), Jack and Ennis evoke tropes of femininity and masculinity."[9] Jack's hands on his hips in a feminine manner in the first few minutes of the film, which leads to that knowingly flirty smirk, and Ennis' tough way of presenting his arm-folded nonchalantness that screams, "I'm a butch man!" Ennis shows his more violent masculinism with Jack in the heat of passion, but also at a Fourth of July event in front of his family – while Jack is more playful, dreams big out loud, and nearly floats around the campground when with Ennis.

Mainstream audiences were able to say, okay, Ennis is *the man* and Jack is *the woman*; I understand that dynamic, and it made the film – the queer film – more palatable for those who lived their non-homosexual middle-America lives. Boucher and Pinto tell it as, "Jack and Ennis made sense, not because they were queer, but because their gendered coupling was and is so familiar."[10] It was brilliant acting and inventive direction that made two supposedly straight-acting good ol' country boys appear simultaneously as those masculine cowboys but also as a sort-of-heterosexualized and easier-to-relate-to mas-culine and feminine couple.

## The Gay Gaze?

When it comes to a perfect example of femininity and *the gaze*, one must look no further than the 1962 film *Cleo from 5 to 7,* directed by Agnés Varda and starring Corinne Marchand. In that film, *the male gaze*, as coined by Laura Mulvey, is easy to spot and under-stand as the film audience sees Cleo walking down the street with the camera panning to the reaction of the crowd around her as they, at times, literally have their mouth agape while they stare at this beautiful idealized version of a woman. So, without a gorgeous female lead to swoon over in *Brokeback Mountain* and the objects of our affection, both strapping and ex-tremely handsome men, does one consider the shots, glances, and lingering moments in the same way? Would the way we are asked to look at Ennis and Jack in this film be considered *the male gaze,* or would it potentially be something more attuned to being called *the gay gaze?*

Clifton Snider claims that *Brokeback Mountain* " . . . breaks ground in a way I have not seen discussed heretofore in the terms of 'gaze' . . . this gaze is dual; in fact, it belongs to the target audience: heterosexual women and gay men."[11] So, how exactly does *the gay gaze* Snider describes differ from *the male gaze* that Mulvey coined? She described the *male gaze* in her article as: " the male gaze projects its fantasy onto the female figure, which is styled accordingly . . . women are simultaneously looked at and displayed, with their appearance coded for strong visual and erotic impact."[12] In *Brokeback Mountain*, there are many moments where *the gaze* (fitting closely to Mulvey's description – only with a man swapped for a woman) can be noted.

This type of gaze, similar to Mulvey's *male gaze*, comes into play in most of the scenes where Jack and Ennis are shirtless and rolling around together – and the most glaring example of this type of gawking gaze at the ripped male form is when Jack is seen washing his clothes in the river and the camera starts with a close-up and then zooms out to a medium shot to show his fully naked body exposed and glistening in the sunlight. Mulvey says shots like this (usually with women) are meant to " . . . freeze the flow of action in moments of erotic contemplation."[13] Ang Lee lets the audience linger on the body of Jack just long enough to think sexy thoughts – but not to interrupt the progression of the film for too long.

If there is a *gay gaze*, it is different from the overtly sexualized and patriarchal version of Mulvey's *male gaze* because it is more than just erotic pleasure that gay men are looking at (or for) in these images of the two gay cowboys on the screen. Snider explains that "as gay gazers, we can appreciate these two young men for who they are, not for whom we'd like them to be, as in the case with other mainstream movies. For once, we and our sympathetic heterosexual sisters are bearers of the look."[14] *Brokeback Mountain*, then, was one of the first mainstream films where the gay male audience did not have to project a homosexual imagination or code onto a heterosexual character to fantasize about – because, finally, there were representations of gay men on the big screen that one could simply look at and enjoy. Finally, in *Brokeback Mountain*, what one saw was what one got, not what one had to create in the mind's eye.

## Middle America Marketing

Brokeback Mountain's journey to becoming a mainstream hit was indeed a remarkable one. Before it graced the screens of New York City, Los Angeles, and Middle America, it earned its stripes as a film festival darling, taking home the prestigious Golden Lion Award at the Venice Film Festival. Ang Lee's acceptance speech for this award served as the blueprint for the marketing team's strategy to make the film more accessible to a broader audience by, in essence, "un-queering" it. Lee told reporters that the film was a "great American love story" that was "unique and so universal."[15]

With a string of festival wins under its belt and a growing buzz surrounding its impending release across the United States, the film's marketing team shifted into high gear to create pre-viewing expectations in the marketplace. This strategy was astutely highlighted by Snider, who referred to a New York Times article where the word "universal" made another appearance in a review. The review stated, "Ennis's and Jack's acute emotions – yearning, loneliness, disappointment, loss, love, and, yes, lust – are affecting because they are universal."[16] The concept of universality became the central pillar of the film's promotion.

Even Heath Ledger, one of the film's stars, underscored this idea in an interview when he remarked that "the level of intimacy and the level of love they experience is the same as that we would experience as heterosexual people... their love does transcend all."[17] With such convincing, widespread marketing that struck a chord with audiences and was substantiated by the film's undeniable emotional depth, it came as no surprise that Brokeback Mountain became a monumental hit.

In retrospect, the film's journey from an indie darling to a mainstream success underscores the transformative power of storytelling. Brokeback Mountain bridged gaps by emphasizing the universal aspects of love, longing, and heartbreak and ignited conversations about the nature of human emotions and relationships. Its enduring impact reminds us that when authenticity and empathy are at the core of a narrative, it has the potential to resonate with audiences across diverse backgrounds, challenging societal norms and fostering a deeper understanding of the human experience.

## *Last Ride: Closing*

No matter how you spin it, Brokeback Mountain is a queer film about queer love and queer heartbreak – and it impacted the lives of many viewers. Boucher and Pinto said it poignantly when they wrote: " . . . representations such as Brokeback Mountain are important for their potential to produce and police meaning in everyday life."[18] This movie touched my life and the lives of many other gay men who finally saw themselves and their relationships on screen for the first time in mainstream movie theaters. Even with all the un-queering attempts made by the film-makers, nothing could ever change the beautiful consequences of Brokeback Mountain when it came out or the lasting impact it continues to have in the current-day gay community and will have for many generations to come.

Brokeback Mountain serves as a testament to the power of storytelling in reshaping societal perceptions and fostering empathy. It broke through barriers, pushing boundaries and challenging stereotypes, ultimately bridging the gap between different communities and offering a glimpse into the complexities of human emotions. As we reflect on this cinematic masterpiece, it reminds us that love transcends gender and societal norms, and it reaffirms the importance of representation in the media. Brokeback Mountain will forever stand as a symbol of progress, leaving an indelible mark on the LGBTQ+ movement and influencing how we approach love and acceptance narratives. It's a reminder that, despite the challenges and discrimination that persist, the power of love and the impact of authentic storytelling can never be denied or extinguished.

## References

[5] Bersani, Leo. "5. Aggression, Gay Shame, and Almodó-var's Art" In *Is the Rectum a Grave?: and Other Essays*, 63-82. Chicago: University of Chicago Press, 2009. https://doi.org/10.7208/9780226043449-006

[2,9,10,17,18] Boucher, Leigh, and Sarah Pinto. 2007. ""I Ain't Queer": Love, Masculinity And History In Brokeback Mountain". *The Journal Of Men's Studies* 15 (3): 311-330. doi:10.3149/jms.1503.311.

"Brokeback Mountain (2005) - IMDb". 2022. *IMDb*. https://www.imdb.com/title/tt0388795/.

[15] "'Brokeback Mountain' Big Winner In Venice". 2022. *TODAY.Com*. https://www.today.com/pop-culture/brokeback-mountain-big-winner-venice-wbna9285873.

[3] Lee, Ang. 2005. Brokeback Mountain. United States: Focus Features

[1,6,7] McBride, Dwight A. 2007. "WHY I HATE THAT I LOVED BROKEBACK MOUNTAIN." *GLQ* 13 (1): 95–97. https://doi.org/10.1215/10642684-2006-016.

Moore, M., 2022. *The Money Behind the 2006 Marriage Amendments - FollowTheMoney.org.*

https://www.followthemoney.org/research/institute-reports/the-money-behind-the-2006-marriage-amendments

[12,13] Mulvey, L. 1975. "Visual Pleasure And Narrative Cinema". *Screen* 16 (3). doi:10.1093/screen/16.3.6.

[4] Reeves, T., 2022. *Filming Locations for Brokeback Mountain (2005), in Alberta, Canada.* The Worldwide Guide to Movie Locations. http://movie-locations.com/movies/b/Brokeback-Mountain.php

[8,11,14,16] Snider, Clifton. 2008. "Queer Persona and the Gay Gaze in Brokeback Mountain: Story and Film." Psychological Perspectives 51 (1): 54–69. https://doi.org/10.1080/00332920802031888.

# Chapter 13

# Audible Pleasure and Character Cinema

**Audible Pleasure and Character Cinema:**
*Stereophilia and the Seductive and Stereotypical
Sound of Female Characters in Film*

Friday, 8th of December, 2023
MPhil in Film and Screen Studies
Core-Course Essay

*Scan the QR Codes in this essay to play the sounds
and videos mentioned.*

## Audible Pleasure and Character Cinema:
### *Stereophilia and the Seductive and Stereotypical Sound of Female Characters in Film*

If you have taken a film studies class any time in the last fifty years, then you will have, more than likely, read Laura Mulvey's "Visual Pleasure and Narrative Cinema." Mulvey wrote this essay in 1975 with a goal and a drive brought on by second-wave feminism and its fight for equality and against discrimination.[1] Two years before she released this work, Roe V. Wade[2] was passed in the United States Congress; the bill found state regulation of abortion illegal, and Title IX[3] passed a year before, made clear that no person, on the basis of sex, could be denied benefits or discriminated against in any educational program that received funds from the government. Fired up by the movement, Mulvey says, in an interview in 2011, that she wrote this often-cited piece through the lens of feminism and that it is a reflection on the time in which it was written. Mulvey also agrees in this interview that she could have considered additional *gazes* and different groups of spectators in her writing.[4] Her willingness to go back, question, and add additional context over the years to her own words[5], which have become the go-to introductory essay for just about every film studies class, is what inspired this essay. What else might be missing from her important but now, considering her revisionary comments since its publication, provisional article?

By contributing novel ideas inspired by Mulvey's own words, in an attempt to help create a more modern interpretation of Mulvey's original work, this essay aims to fill in some gaps that Mulvey and other scholars have claimed could have been added to her seminal article when it was originally published. Mulvey's laser-eyed focus on *the look* and Freudian psychoanalysis[6] bypasses the invisible but related sounds, accents, vocal ranges, and tonal styles women characters (and their actors) were expected to make to create an audible pleasure to go with the visual. This essay, focusing on a curiosity about female sound in cinema, will be explored through a close viewing of *and listening* to Alfred Hitchcock's *Vertigo* while also touching on more recent films and television shows like Tina Fey's *Mean Girls* and Fran Dresher's *The Nanny*. This essay will highlight contributions from scholars such as Kaja Silverman and Britta Sjogren, who have enriched the discourse on sound in film while also refining and expanding upon Mulvey's original concept. Additionally, it will incorporate scientific data from *The Journal of Social and Personal Relationships*, as well as Laura Mulvey's reflections through essays and interviews spanning the decades since the inception of her theory.

Figure 1. Kim Novak as Madeleine
in Hitchcock's Vertigo.

## Stereophilia: Audible Pleasure

A look can say so much without words. Just stare into Kim Novak's eyes in character as Madeleine in *Vertigo* (figure 1) for a moment, and one could imagine her thoughts, intentions, or the fantasies of a person at the end of her gaze, which might be running through her mind. One might even assign a particular type of voice to this look in one's own imagination. The voice of seduction: a single-sourced audible erotic vibration of feminine humanity that pulsates through the vocal cords of the actress and brings her character to life. So, how does one create this voice? How does the audience know what to expect? And how does the actress know which vocality to use for each character she plays? In this essay, we will call it *Stereophilia*.

Stereophilia, akin to Freud's idea of scopophilia, "where looking itself is a source of pleasure," is the circumstance in which *listening* itself is a source of pleasure.[7] As Laura Mulvey explains, Freud " . . . associated scopophilia with taking other people as objects, subjecting them to a controlling and curious gaze."[8] This idea from Freud could then, in turn, be applied to the controlling ways in which cinema has pigeon-holed female characters into certain stereotypical and expected sounds. The concept of stereophilia goes far beyond film and can be found in many forms of media, including television, radio, and social media.

## *Stereophilia: Pleasurable Stereotypes in Sound*

Figure 2. Kim Novak as Madeleine awakens in Scottie's apartment in Hitchcock's *Vertigo*. Cinematography by Robert Burkes.

In *Vertigo*, the voice Kim Novak uses, the voice of the character, is not her own; it is Madeleine's voice (figure 2). The accent, sound, and tone chosen for this character connect seamlessly and naturally in a manner that Kaja Silverman calls "general compatibility of voice and body,"[9] and it is specifically selected for this role and this character. She has a voice that invites you to move in closer, her soft alto, nearly mono-tonal vocality that lulls one into an audible realm of safety and seduction. Silverman uses a scene from *Singing in the Rain* (figure 3), another studio-era film from the 1950s, to explain this unconscious expectation of the compatibility from body to voice:

"You're a beautiful woman; audiences think you have a voice to match," explains a publicist to silent screen star Lina Lamon in the film *Singin' in the Rain* (1952) when she wonders why she's not allowed to answer the questions directed to her by fans and reporters. Lina (Jean Hagen) violates this expectation of smooth complementarity whenever she opens her mouth; she speaks shrilly and ungrammatically, with a heavy Bronx accent. The studio for which she works, Monumental Pictures, attempts to conceal the seeming heterogeneity of her voice to her body by having others speak for her.[10]

This concept that a voice should match a body, no doubt, has its origins in the patriarchal status quo that Mulvey and other film scholars have pointed to for decades. The idea is that a

Figure 3. Jean Hagan as Lina Lamont in Singing in the Rain (1952) surrounded by men, one of whom is her publicist.[8]

specific type of woman should look a certain way and that a particular kind of woman should sound a certain way, too, whether explicitly written in a script or by the suggestion of a director or not. When Mulvey stated, " . . . mainstream film coded the erotic into the language of the dominant patriarchal order,"[11] she was focused on the visual language and not the *spoken language*, which we now argue goes hand in hand with the visual stereotyping, expectations, and constraints forced upon female characters in studio-era cinema and that continues into the mainstream cinema of today.

The voices chosen for each character can, and often do, reflect their socioeconomic status as well. In *Vertigo*, Kim Novak also plays a character named Judy, and the voice she uses for that role is different – less polished and more middle-class. Madeleine, Kim's character as the audience knows her in the first half of the film, is married to a businessman comfortable with money, and she comes from a wealthy family herself.

Her voice is smooth with crisp consonants at the end of words and could be categorized as Transatlantic or Mid-Atlantic[12], which is almost a British accent without actually being British. Judy has a more relaxed tone and trails off at the ends of words, with no crisp consonants to finish her vocalized thoughts (figure 4 at 2:00 minutes into the clip).

Figure 4. Kim Novak as Judy in Hitchcock's *Vertigo*. Cinematography by Robert Burkes.

What is it about a voice that brings a listening spectator the desired audio pleasure that aligns with the conceptual framework of stereophila? Science tells us that it is our brain, the auditory cortex and the amygdala, to be exact, making connections and memories to sounds that either please us or are unpleasant to us.[13] Fingernails on a blackboard are often pinned at the top of the list of worst sounds to the human listener, according to *The Journal of Science*, and on the opposite aural spectrum, "many people find natural environmental soundscapes (ocean waves, rainfall, etc.) to be relaxing and pleasant."[14] Psychology, though, also specifically links the sounds a mother makes to her child in the womb and during infancy as the basis for what we find pleasing when it comes to our female cinematic characters, as Kaja Silverman explores in her book, "The Acoustic Mirror: The Female Voice in Psychoanalysis and Cinema." She speaks to the fantasy of the mother's voice as the "[ . . . ] maternal-voice-as-sonorous-envelope [ . . . ] viewed from the site of the unconscious, the image of the infant held within the environment or sphere of the mother's voice is an emblem of infantile plentitude and bliss,"[15] which re-engages the wants and needs of listening spectators to seek out that long-lost comfort.

In 2015, researchers Susan M. Hughes and Noelle E. Miller from Albright College in the United States of America conducted an experiment to better understand the human mind's correlation of attractiveness or unattractiveness between voices and faces. Their study entitled, "What sounds beautiful looks beautiful stereotype: The matching of attractiveness of voices and faces," resulted in findings that showed "that there was an overall tendency to associate attractive voices with attractive faces and unattractive voices with unattractive faces, suggesting that a 'what-sounds-beautiful-looks-beautiful' stereotype exists."[16] Their research leans towards solidifying the theory that stereophilia, the pleasure derived from listening, played a part in the creation of early and studio-era cinema, whether casting directors, directors, or actors realized they were fully or intentionally subscribing to it. Perhaps casting directors did subconsciously already know what Hughes and Miller reported in their research:

It has been shown that women generally perceive high-pitched male voices to be unattractive [ . . . ] and prefer deeper male voices, while men perceive higher-pitched female voices as sounding more attractive [ . . . ]. On the other hand, Daniel and McCabe (1992) found that mid-pitched voices for both sexes sounded the "most sexy," suggesting that voices with pitches that deviated too far from the average (within each sex's average voice pitch range) could indicate hormonal abnormalities[17]

Many researchers have been studying this theory since at least the early 2000s, but clearly, the idea of matching an attractive voice to an attractive face has been in the minds of cinematic producers and practitioners for many decades prior, as seen in the *Singing in the Rain* example provided earlier in this essay.

While not quite finger-nails on a blackboard or particularly motherly, one could look at *and listen to* Fran Dresher's character in the television show *The Nanny* to understand how a voice that does

Figure 5. Fran Dresher's character, Fran Fine, meets Fran Dresher the actor in *The Nanny* season 6, episode 20.

not quite match the body can successfully navigate the framework pitfalls of stereophilia. The character and those around her often engage in commentary about her voice, highlighting its misalignment by either self-deprecating humor or playful, friendly jabs, respectively. The Nanny was an incredibly successful show, and in the second to last episode of the series, the nanny character meets the actor Fran Dresher in a hotel, and they briefly discuss her voice in a funny yet telling moment. The Nanny character states, "Oh my god, you really do talk like that," and Fran replies, "Who would make this up?" (figure 5).

This discussion on pleasant-sounding voices that match attractive looks begs the question: is this theory more applicable to or more often expected of female characters in film? When it comes to movies like *Vertigo*, it appears that deriving pleasure from listening, from the character of Madeleine most specifically, was paramount when it came to choosing the voice and accents that were used. The film centers around Madeleine as the object of desire, consistent with Mulvey's idea of the gaze[18], and choosing a voice that gives the listening spectator pleasure was integral to the film's success. Hughes and Miller stated, "It is believed that the attractiveness of the voice and face is especially related to women as both may signal common underlying cues of desired femininity."[19] Therefore, for Madeleine, representing grace, beauty, class, and femininity, aligning the most appealing voice was crucial.

Figure 6. Kim Novak speaks to the British Film Institute about her experience working on Hitchcock's *Vertigo*.

Then, when we first meet Judy Barton in *Vertigo*, and we hear her unpolished voice and see her mousy brown hair, we, as listening spectators meant to identify with Scottie, are taken aback. Not only did the film's producers, costumers, and makeup designers dress Kim Novak down and give her brown and looser hair as Judy, but they also changed her voice. This choice was, no doubt, an intentional one by Hitchcock to make the audience an accomplice in the desire to see Judy change back into Madeleine in both dress, demeanor, and vocality. In a 2012 interview with the British Film Institute, Kim Novak tells us that Hitchcock "knew exactly what he wanted." Novak says that she saw herself as Judy "trying to become the Hollywood person" by imitating the look and sounds of the leading lady figures of the time that she admired and aspired to be (figure 6).[20]

Cinema and television of the 2000s and beyond, while much more diverse in visual representations found in mainstream hits, still fall prey to the stereotyping of female characters in relation to their vocal ranges and outputs. In *Mean Girls (2004)*, female characters are the narrators and control the storyline, while the central object of desire in the film is the lead male character named Aaron. This film has the framework of a project that might have made 1975 Laura Mulvey add a slightly different take to her original piece, but the movie still falls into the culturally entrenched tropes of stereotyping a female sound to a look. Each of the three *Plastics* (Regina, Gretchen, and Karen) has a distinct voice that matches the characters they are representing in the world of the film, and when the women all meet for the first time, it is clear to determine by looks and voice, the role each one plays in the popularity paradigm (figure 7).

Regina, the equivalent of *Vertigo*'s Madeleine, the blonde Queen Bee, has an updated version of the Transatlantic accent with a sultry lower-range soprano tone. Gretchen, the mousy brown-haired sidekick, Regina's number

Figure 7. *The Plastics*, Karen played by Amanda Seyfried. Regina played by Rachel McAdams, and Gretchen played by Lacey Chabert, sit across from Cady played by Lindsay Lohan in the North Shore High School cafeteria as they introduce themselves in Tina Fey's *Mean Girls*. Cinematography by Daryn Okada.

two, has more of a loose and, at times, squeaky tone to her voice, which is reminiscent of Judy in *Vertigo*. The listening spectator is supposed to find Gretchen physically and vocally attractive but not as attractive as Regina. Karen, the number three to Regina, also a blonde with looks comparable to the Queen Bee, has a valley-girl-breathy-whimsical voice that is meant to detract from her looks by associating her voice with unintelligence. By making the character of Karen sound dull-witted, the filmmakers once again turn the spectators' eyes and ears back to Regina. Cady, who eventually becomes the Queen Bee in the second half of the film, experiences a transition in her voice from start to finish. Initially, Cady is a very quiet and shy-sounding girl who, after changing her look, becomes one with a reverberant and smooth alto voice that the listening spectator has come to expect from their lead female characters. The vocal choices for these leading ladies did not start at the actor or even the director. Often, it is in the screenplay where one finds the beginnings of the coherence to the stereotyped female voice that listening spectators have come to expect from female characters in film and television.

## *Stereophilia: From Script to Sound to Screen*

In the last half of this essay on female character voices in cinema, we will look at *and listen* to sound directions written in film scripts that initiate the cycle of stereophilia before an actor even speaks the words in front of a camera. Britta Sjogren states that "it takes a lot of effort to create sounds for film" and that "through these tools, these apparatuses, sound is worked, directed, and manipulated; in a sense, sound is more frequently consciously crafted than the visual image."[21] The journey to cinematic stereophilia begins with the script. First, let us return to the scene in *Vertigo* where Madeleine has woken up in Scottie's apartment, naked and in his bed, now sitting in the living room, warming by the fire in a robe he has given her. In the script, on page 52[22], Scottie continues questioning Madeleine about where she had been earlier in the day, and Madeleine begins to respond to him playfully. From a listening spectator's vantage point who has never seen the script, one might assume the choices made in vocal character were fully those of the actor or director, but one comes to understand by reading the screenplay that the writers had imagined this sound prior to filming.

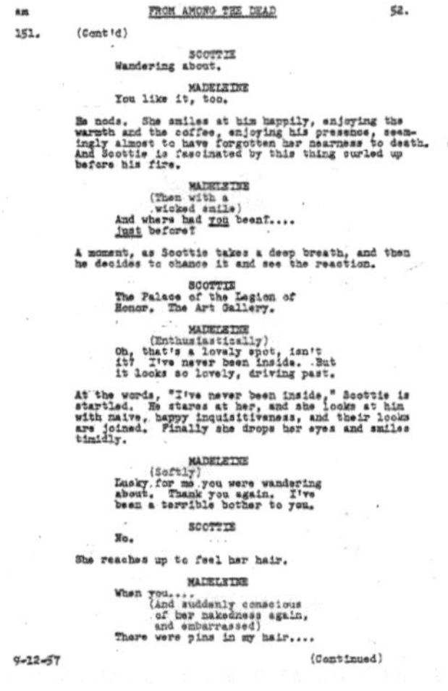

Figure 8. Page 52 from the *Vertigo* screenplay
written by Alec Coppel, Samuel Taylor, and Hitchcock

On this one page of the script (figure 8), we see four vocal directions written for the female character and none for the male character. From this perspective, it appears that the writers Alec Coppel, Samuel Taylor, and Alfred Hitchcock felt it necessary to prescribe the female actor multiple directions to encounter when she initially read the script before production began. This action and these directions were meant to ignite her imagination to create the voice they wished to produce for the film which would, in turn, produce the most audible pleasure for the listening spectator. The audience that Mulvey argued, at the time, was undoubtedly heterosexual and male-centric[23] and would have appreciated the male screenplay writers and the male director's encouragement of their female lead to produce a seductive vocal attractiveness when in character as Madeleine. After watching and listening to the film, they could then hold on to the memory of this unattainable and angelic-looking and sounding creature that they could fantasize about long after they left the theatre.

Mulvey in conversation with Roberta Sassatelli in 2011, revisits her thoughts on male-centric spectatorship in "Interview with Laura Mulvey: Gender, Gaze, and Technology in Film Culture" and questions what a female spectator might have gleaned from these types of images. Mulvey reflectively states that "although the textual approach stands [in "Visual Pleasure and Narrative Cinema"], there are also multiple audiences and spectator positions, multiple ways in which different kinds of social groups are distanced, or entranced by the images on screen."[24] Mulvey's willingness to return to and ruminate over the potential evolution of her early theory with an open mind, created new avenues for discussion. Even with years of new context added about different gazes and spectators, in the 2011 interview both Mulvey and Roberta Sassatelli overlooked the opportunity to explore the *sounds* that female listening spectators might have experienced and how it could have impacted their lives.[25]

*Imitation is the sincerest form of flattery*, the immortal and globally recognized phrase often attested to Oscar Wilde, seems to neatly summarise what it means to be a listening spectator influenced by film and media. On page 16 of the *Mean Girls* script[26], we see more vocal commands written for the female characters. This time, the instructions are written by a woman, Tina Fey, but they still play into the vocal stereotypes found in studio-era cinema. *Disdainful,* here (figure 9), is not just a feeling or emotion, in this context, it is a vocal directive meant to evoke a different pitch from the character with, perhaps, a guttural growl of disgust attached to the utterance.

The following direction, *withering*, is a term one may use to describe the death of a plant or flower, but in this case, it is used to arouse a vocal wilt and retreat. Gretchen is initially so proud of her interjection, "That's so fetch," but is immediately torn down emotionally by just three words spoken with an inflection only the Queen Bees of cinema are allowed to use.

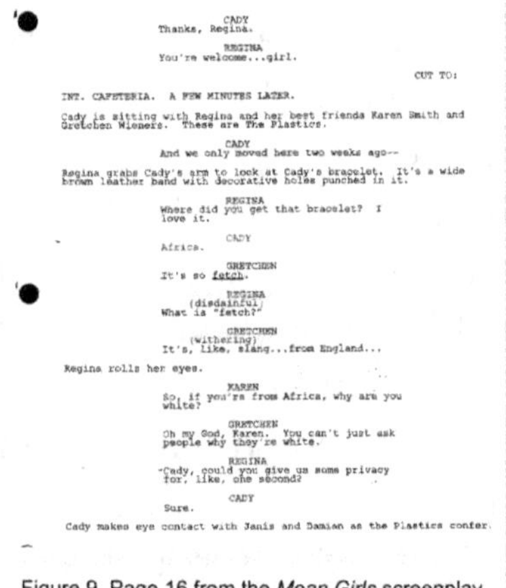


Figure 9. Page 16 from the *Mean Girls* screenplay written by Tina Fey

Although Regina annihilated any chance that the word *fetch* would ever become part of the characters' in-film lexicon, the word did have a global impact on the film's millions of listening spectators. Instead of becoming a word that people used to mean what Gretchen had intended, that something *fetch* was *cool*, the greater population of listening spectators did use the word quite frequently but to an opposite effect, becoming "the antithesis of cool."[27] And while *fetch* did not become a global linguistic phenomenon, the fact that a large number of young girls and women were using quotes and phrases from the film and mimicking both clothing styles and vocal expressions confirms just how powerful the visual *and sound* choices made in cinema truly are.

## Conclusion

Britta Sjogren captured the idea of this essay perfectly when she wrote, "sound and voice [ . . .] are more frequently viewed as cosmetic appendixes to the more primary constructing power of image [ . . . ] But the contribution of voice and sound to the articulation of point of view 'of' a text or character, in fact, is anything but secondary."[28]

In conclusion, this essay has aimed to address and augment the insights of Laura Mulvey's seminal work, "Visual Pleasure and Narrative Cinema," by focusing on the often-overlooked dimension of sound, specifically the voices of female characters in cinema. Inspired by Mulvey's own acknowledgment of potential gaps in her theory, this essay explored the concept of Stereophilia, arguing that the pleasure derived from listening is a crucial yet understudied aspect of cinematic experience.

By delving into the close viewing of Alfred Hitchcock's *Vertigo* and drawing on perspectives from scholars such as Kaja Silverman and Britta Sjogren, the essay highlighted the significant role of female voices in shaping listening spectator's perceptions. The analysis extended beyond Mulvey's original theory to consider the auditory dimensions of cinema, questioning the stereotypical expectations placed on female characters' voices and their alignment with societal ideals of femininity. In revisiting Mulvey's exploration of heterosexual male-centric spectatorship, the essay also pointed to the evolving landscape of film reception and opens the door to more considerations of the impact cinematic sounds have on other categories of listening spectators.

This essay also incorporated scientific findings, such as the correlation between attractive voices and faces, as demonstrated by the research of Susan M. Hughes and Noelle E. Miller. It argued that the intentional selection of voices for female characters, as exemplified in *Vertigo*, reflects broader societal expectations and reinforces stereotypical norms.

Furthermore, the essay explored how sound directions in film scripts contribute to the perpetuation of stereotypical female voices even before actors bring the characters to life on screen. This examination suggests that the production process, from scriptwriting to directing, plays a pivotal role in shaping stereophilia, the auditory pleasure, experienced by the audience: the listening spectators.

By acknowledging the importance of sound in cinema, and specifically the voices of female characters, this essay contributes to a more comprehensive understanding of the audiovisual dynamics that influence audience perceptions and enjoyment. In doing so, it underscores the need for continued exploration and reevaluation of cinematic theories to encompass the multifaceted nature of the cinematic experience.

## Bibliography

[20]British Film Institute. 2012. *Kim Novak on Vertigo.* https://www.youtube.com/watch?v=0Im8wCTSCw4.

[12]Drum, Kevin. 2011. "Oh, That Old-Timey Movie Accent!" Mother Jones. August 9, 2011. https://www.motherjones.com/kevin-drum/2011/08/oh-old-timey-movie-voice/.

[16,19] Hughes, Susan M, and Noelle E Miller. "What Sounds Beautiful Looks Beautiful Stereotype." *Journal of Social and Personal Relationships* 33, no. 7 (2016): 984.

Jacobson, Peter Marc, dir. 2021. *Fran Meets Fran Drescher! | The Nanny.* The Nanny | YouTube. https://www.youtube.com/watch?v=v0IEAGi2K1M.

[27]Making "Fetch" Happen: What Makes New Words Catch On?, GRETCHEN MCCULLOCH, 2104. https://slate.com/human-interest/2014/05/mean-girls-slang-fetch-10-years-later-why-it-didn-t-catch-on-according-to-predicting-new-words-by-linguist-allan-metcalf.html

[14]McDermott, Josh H. "Chapter 10 - Auditory Preferences and Aesthetics: Music, Voices, and Everyday

Sounds." In *Neuroscience of Preference and Choice*, 227-56. Elsevier, 2012.

"Mean Girls (1/10) Movie Clip - Meeting the Plastics (2004) HD." 2011. October 7, 2011. https://www.youtube.com/watch?v=re5veV2F7eY.

[6,7,8,11,18,23,] Mulvey, Laura. "Visual Pleasure and Narrative Cinema." *Screen (London)* 16, no. 3 (1975): 6-18.

[5] Mulvey, Laura. "AFTERTHOUGHTS ON 'VISUAL PLEASURE AND NARRATIVE CINEMA' INSPIRED BY 'DUEL IN THE SUN' (KING VIDOR, 1946)." *Framework* 15-17, no. 15/17 (1981): 12-15.

[2] "Roe v. Wade." 2023. Encyclopædia Britannica. Encyclopædia Britannica, inc. December 7, 2023. https://www.britannica.com/event/Roe-v-Wade.

[1, 4, 24, 25] Sassatelli, Roberta. "Interview with Laura Mulvey." *Theory, Culture & Society* 28, no. 5 (2011): 123-43.

"Scottie Meets Brunette Judy/Madeleine in Her Apartment - Vertigo Remastered (1958)." 2021. YouTube. Cringe Cook. March 10, 2021. https://www.youtube.com/watch?v=ZmLB4xtNtTc.

[9,10,15]Silverman, Kaja. *Acoustic Mirror, The.* Bloomington: Indiana University Press, 1988.

*Singing in the Rain - Opponent* . LPKvideoDesigns Youtube. 2014. https://www.youtube.com/watch?v=G4-GetMScLg.

[21,28]Sjogren, Britta H. *Into the Vortex.* 1st ed. Champaign: University of Illinois Press, 2006.

[13]Sukhbinder Kumar, Katharina von Kriegstein, Karl Friston, Timothy D. Griffiths. "Features versus Feelings: Dissociable Representations of the Acoustic Features and Valence of Aversive Sounds." *Journal of Neuroscience* 10 October 2012, 32 (41) 14184-14192;

[3]"Title IX." 2023. Encyclopædia Britannica. Encyclopædia Britannica, inc. December 6, 2023. https://www.britannica.com/event/Title-IX.

"Vertigo (4/11) Movie Clip - What Happened? (1958) HD." 2011. YouTube. Movieclips. May 28, 2011. https://www.youtube.com/watch?v=ZruKu2N6nQw.

[17] For further investigation on other studies and experiments on this specific research topic, check out: Riding, D., Lonsdale, D., & Brown, B. (2006). The Effects of Average Fundamental Frequency

and Variance of Fundamental Frequency on Male Vocal Attractiveness to Women. Journal of Nonverbal Behavior, 30(2), 55–61, by Collins, S. A., & Missing, C. (2003). Vocal and visual attractiveness are related in women. Animal Behaviour, 65(5), 997–1004., and Jones, B.C. , Debruine, L.M. , Little, A.C., Conway, C.A. and Feinberg, D.R. (2006) Integrating gaze direction and expression in preferences for attractive faces. *Psychological Science*, 17(7), pp. 588-591.

[22,26]A full-page print of this script page can be found after the bibliography for closer viewing

151.      (Cont'd)

                         SCOTTIE
                    Wandering about.

                         MADELEINE
                    You like it, too.

He nods.  She smiles at him happily, enjoying the
warmth and the coffee, enjoying his presence, seem-
ingly almost to have forgotten her nearness to death.
And Scottie is fascinated by this thing curled up
before his fire.

                         MADELEINE
                         (Then with a
                         wicked smile)
                    And where had you been?....
                    just before?

A moment, as Scottie takes a deep breath, and then
he decides to chance it and see the reaction.

                         SCOTTIE
                    The Palace of the Legion of
                    Honor.  The Art Gallery.

                         MADELEINE
                         (Enthusiastically)
                    Oh, that's a lovely spot, isn't
                    it?  I've never been inside.  But
                    it looks so lovely, driving past.

At the words, "I've never been inside," Scottie is
startled.  He stares at her, and she looks at him
with naive, happy inquisitiveness, and their looks
are joined.  Finally she drops her eyes and smiles
timidly.

                         MADELEINE
                         (Softly)
                    Lucky for me you were wandering
                    about.  Thank you again.  I've
                    been a terrible bother to you.

                         SCOTTIE
                    No.

She reaches up to feel her hair.

                         MADELEINE
                    When you....
                         (And suddenly conscious
                         of her nakedness again,
                         and embarrassed)
                    There were pins in my hair....

9-12-57                                        (Continued)

                              CADY
          Thanks, Regina.

                              REGINA
          You're welcome...girl.

                                                  CUT TO:


INT. CAFETERIA.  A FEW MINUTES LATER.

Cady is sitting with Regina and her best friends Karen Smith and
Gretchen Wieners.  These are The Plastics.

                              CADY
          And we only moved here two weeks ago--

Regina grabs Cady's arm to look at Cady's bracelet.  It's a wide
brown leather band with decorative holes punched in it.

                              REGINA
          Where did you get that bracelet?  I
          love it.

                              CADY
          Africa.

                              GRETCHEN
          It's so <u>fetch</u>.

                              REGINA
                    (disdainful)
          What is "fetch?"

                              GRETCHEN
                    (withering)
          It's, like, slang...from England...

Regina rolls her eyes.

                              KAREN
          So, if you're from Africa, why are you
          white?

                              GRETCHEN
          Oh my God, Karen.  You can't just ask
          people why they're white.

                              REGINA
          -Cady, could you give us some privacy
          for, like, one second?

                              CADY
          Sure.

Cady makes eye contact with Janis and Damian as the Plastics confer.

# Chapter 14

# TV Pilot: Heartbreak Dreams

*Written in the Harvard Course:*

*Advanced TV Writing: The One-Hour Drama Pilot and Serialized Storytelling*

*Taught by: Maria Arena Bell & Marla Kanelos*

## HEARTBREAK DREAMS | A TRUE STORY

## "PILOT"

Based on the memoir *Hollywood Heartbreak | New York Dreams This series is so much more than just an adaptation of a memoir - Heartbreak Dreams is a new kind of television show. A true story told through real photos and actor portrayals - a very meta show that breaks many traditional rules. It is a show about the making of a show that has another show within.*

*The protagonist is multifaceted, inspiring, and doesn't quite fit the "normal" Hero mold - but he is the hero of this story. A story of finding oneself and helping others along the way.*

## ACT ONE

## 1    P1-1: INT. SWANKY PENTHOUSE APARTMENT - NEW YORK CITY - LATE NIGHT

OPEN TO: a black screen. We hear the fumbling of keys and the playful noises of hushed, flirty giggles. A thick metal door slides open and a muscular arm can be seen reaching in to flip on the lights.

Sarah and Liam come home in a passionate mood after a night on the town. A beautiful blonde with long flowing hair and bright blue eyes wearing a trench coat and cowboy boots struts in through the metal door of the rock n' roll decorated penthouse apartment of her rock star lover, Liam, (tall, chiseled face and abs, Kurt Cobain hair) who follows right behind as they enter. The apartment has gold records hanging on the wall, tour posters, and a Grammy sits sparkling on his nightstand next to his lamp that looks like a guitar. Liam steps in front to grab Sarah's hand as they continue into the apartment. The sexual tension is clear, we know what is about to take place. Or do we?

SARAH

(giggles)

Well, well, well ... What a night. Did you have fun, mister?

LIAM

(leading Sarah towards the bedroom)

Of course I did, baby. Anytime I get to watch you shake that ass and perform for the crowd is a fun night for me.

(slaps her on the butt as she walks ahead of him)

## 2    P1-2: INT. HALLWAY/BEDROOM/ BATHROOM OF LIAM'S PENTHOUSE APARTMENT

Sarah guides Liam to the bed and heads to the bathroom to undress.

FROM THE HALLWAY TO THE BEDROOM: Sarah once again steps in front to lead Liam to his own bed – the cat and mouse power struggle is a sexy game they play before the passionate inevitable. Liam is gently shoved onto the bed and he loves it – he begins to unbutton his shirt. Sarah gives a coy smile.

STAY WITH SARAH, as she walks to the bathroom door squarely in front of the bed – directly within Liam's view. She looks over her shoulder, hair tossed, smiles, and drops the trench coat she is wearing to reveal a Daisy-Duke-style outfit, then enters the bathroom with one last look and closes the door with her shiny pink boot.

## 3    P1-3: INT. BATHROOM/BEDROOM OF LIAM'S APT - NIGHT

BRITNEY SPEARS "BREATHE ON ME" plays in the background.

START ON SARAH IN THE BATHROOM, looking into the mirror, then PAN DOWN to boots as she takes them off.

CUT TO:

LIAM is on the bed, taking off his shoes.

CUT TO:

SARAH as she peels off her cut-off jean shorts.

CUT TO:

LIAM wiggles out of his pants.

CUT TO:

SARAH unclasping her bra and dropping it to the floor.

CUT TO:

LIAM takes off his shirt, revealing his six-pack abs and big chest.

CUT TO:

SARAH as the camera pans from her back to her right arm – the arm disappears from camera then returns to frame holding a blonde wig, the wig is set delicately on a shelf.

CUT TO:

LIAM fixing his hair and trying to get into a sexy pose on the bed.

CUT TO:

SARAH head down in the sink washing her face – finally looking back into the mirror to reveal Sarah is actually Kaleb Klein, a good-looking, smooth young man with dark brown hair and the same sparkling blue eyes. Kaleb takes off his underwear and wraps himself in a towel ready to head back out to the bedroom where Liam awaits.

## 4     P1-4: INT. BEDROOM OF LIAM'S APT - NIGHT

START ON KALEB in the bathroom doorway, standing in nothing but a small towel, smiling at Liam, who is now naked on the bed. Kaleb and Liam have passionate sex (Liam clearly knew Sarah was Kaleb), and once they are done, Kaleb cuddles up into the spot under Liam's arm, commonly known as "the nook," where he feels safe and loved.

LIAM
Damn, baby. That was hot as fuck.
Kissing Liam on the chin
KALEB
Damn, mister. You are hot as fuck.
Liam kisses Kaleb on the forehead.
LIAM
I'm so glad we made this work. You are like no one I have ever been with before - you fucking make me a better man. I love you, Kaleb.
With a huge smile and peace.
KALEB
I love you too, Liam. I love you, too....

His eyes close and we FADE TO BLACK and...
CUT TO:

# 5    P1-5: EXT. DIRTY NEW YORK CITY ALLEYWAY – EARLY MORNING

FADE IN:

CLOSE UP, we find Kaleb's face in the same angle as the dream – but as we PAN OUT, we see his face is much worse for wear, dirty, and his hair is a mess. He has kept himself comfortable that night on the streets of NYC by using a trash bag for a pillow and another as "the nook" of a man who is not there. As he dreams -

KALEB

I love you, too ... I love you, too..

As his eyes slowly open and the waft of the trash's heinous odor reaches his nose, Kaleb looks devastated to realize the whole thing had just been a dream and that his real world is nothing like the visions he had.

KALEB (CONT'D)

(As if he is talking to the trash bag man)

What the fuck?? Where the fuck am I? How in the fuck did I get here?

Kaleb pushes his trash bag boyfriend off of him and he gets up still a bit tipsy and fumbles about to find a piece of paper he must have dropped the night before that says: NYC HOMELESS SHELTERS.

KALEB (CONT'D)

Well, this will be something new...

CUT TO TITLE:

[TITLE SCREEN]

Quick flashes of New York and Los Angeles and the tile:  "HEARTBREAK DREAMS"

6     P2-1: INT. SOUND STAGE - INTERVIEW ROOM - DAY

Kody sits on a soundstage surrounded by lights and tv production equipment. START ON KODY on a couch in what looks to be an interview but he is speaking directly to the camera - breaking the fourth wall it seems).

KODY

Hey, thanks for being here with me. I can't believe I'm actually here getting to tell my life story on tv. It feels like a dream!

(he sits up straighter) So, what I'm going to tell you is the true story of the insane adventures that got me - here today. I'll change all the names, of course, to protect those involved – even though some don't really deserve it. But, before I dive into the story we're really here to talk about... let me just give you a little background on who I am and where I came from.

Kody points to a tv screen behind him and the camera zooms in as we fade into a memory montage with VO.

## 7      P2-2: MAP TO SMALL TOWN (MAP)

The CAMERA ZOOMS from full map of the US down to the town Kody/Kaleb grew up in.
OPEN ON map of USA.
ZOOM to state of Texas.
Then ZOOM TO Dallas/Fort Worth.
Finally ZOOM all the way in to show the small city of Hurst.
CUT TO:

## 8      P2-3 INT. YOUNG KALEB'S HOUSE - DAY

We see a young Kaleb, 5, and his mother in his childhood home.
A young brown-haired, blue-eyed boy with his red headed, tall, and attractive mother who is a nurse (she is wearing scrubs and has a name tag: Ulla). OVER THIS;

KODY (V.O.)
It was just me and my mama back then.
A single mother raising a rambunctious little boy who was destined to endure an adventure of a life. It all started out so innocent...
CUT TO:

## 9    P2-4: INT. KALEB'S HOUSE – MOTHER'S BEDROOM - DAY

We see a young Kaleb playing dress up, pretending to be a girl. The young boy, now 6, has a white shirt on his head to resemble long hair and is seen pulling his mother's shoes out of her closet and trying them on while dancing and singing into a hairbrush. *Tiffany's 'I THINK WE'RE ALONE NOW'* is playing as he dances. OVER THIS;

KODY (V.O.)

I wasn't like all the other little boys in town. I was different... unique. And in Texas, back then, being that kind of "different" was frowned upon.

Kaleb dances and sings along to the Tiffany song.

KALEB

(sung)

I think we're alone now! Doesn't seem to be any-one around. I think we're alone now. The beating of our hearts are the only sound.

CUT TO:

## 10    P2-5A INT. KMART - TOY SECTION - AFTERNOON

*'GIRLS JUST WANT TO HAVE FUN' by Cyndi Lauper* plays on the store's speakers. Kaleb, 6, and Ulla are in Kmart doing a little shopping on one of Ulla's rare days off. Kaleb is basically dragging her to the toy

section where they walk passed the "boy" section and into the "girl" section. Kaleb is an only child and Ulla often gives him what he wants - today she was a bit more hesitant. OVER THIS;

KODY (V.O.)
I learned some lessons sooner than
I had to. But that's how it was in Texas when I was little...
KALEB
(approaching the shelves full of Barbies)
This is the one!
(his eyes light up)
Mom, mom, mom! Look at her! Isn't she the prettiest?
Kaleb picks up the Special Edition Holiday Barbie that is dressed in a sleek and shiny silver dress with flowing blonde hair and blue eyes.
ULLA
Yes, she is very pretty, Kaleb. Maybe we should go check out the boy toys? G.I. Joe? Ninja Turtles? What do you think?
KALEB
I want her! Pleeeeeeeease!!
(he gets on his knees in a very dramatic fashion)
Pleeeeeeeease, mommy.
ULLA
Oh, alright. Get up. Don't make a scene.
KALEB
(jumping up and down in excitement)

Thank you, thank you, thank you! You are the best mom in the wooooorld!

ULLA

(bending down and putting her hands on his shoulders to calm him) Listen, Kaleb. This is a girl's toy, other parents might not get toys like this for their little boys, so maybe for right now, just put it in the basket, okay?

KALEB

(he resists at first) But mommyyyyyyy...

Ulla gives one of her "don't try me kid" looks and Kaleb folds and puts the Barbie into the shopping cart and they move along to the next aisle.

## 11    P2-5B INT. KMART - CHECKOUT COUNTER - AFTERNOON

At the checkout counter a woman is finishing up her purchase and looks back at Kaleb now holding the bright pink Barbie box with a big smile on his face as he waits in line. Ulla is digging for her credit card in her purse and doesn't see the odd look the woman gives Kaleb. He understands what that look means, though, it was the look his mother had warned him about. He was too young to have to say what he said next.

As Ulla and Kaleb get up to the register for their turn and most of their products have been scanned, Ulla motions for him to put the Barbie on the conveyor belt. Kaleb looks up at the cashier.

KALEB

It's for my sister. She's not with us right now. She's at home.

FEMALE CASHIER

Oh, that's very sweet of you.

The cashier gives a smile to Ulla and Ulla gives her a knowing and thankful smile back. The cashier bags the doll in a separate bag and hands it over the counter to Kaleb while Ulla pays and grabs the other bags.

## 12    P2-5C INT. KALEB'S CHILDHOOD BEDROOM - LATE AFTERNOON

*'I SAW THE SIGN' by Ace of Base* plays. Kaleb's room has many different types of toys. There is a pink bouncy ball in the corner, the He-Man castle, GreySkull, and all the characters, but She-Ra is on the top. There are two Ken dolls, minus their clothes. And three Barbies - all blonde with blue eyes. Kaleb has snuck his mother's hair crimper from her bathroom and is playfully attempting to do Barbie's hair. He is alone in his room but he is happy in a space free of judgement. Ulla walks by his room and stops in the doorframe to look at her son. She smiles but it is also clear she worries about him. OVER THIS;

KODY (V.O.)

The signs were pretty clear from the get-go. I liked She-Ra better than He-Man. I chose to play as Barbie over Ken. I wanted to do the things the girls were doing and I was lucky that I had a mother who let me just be me.

## 13    P2-6: INT. KALEB'S CHILDHOOD BEDROOM - LATE NIGHT

Young Kaleb, 7, is fast asleep with his night-light on, his Grandmother ELEONORE (60's, a sweet look-ing, plump, German woman with salt and pepper hair) has fallen asleep on the couch in the living room waiting for Ulla to get home from the hospital. Ulla comes home and rushes into Kaleb's room. She had just seen a teenager die from a heroin overdose. She gently wakes Kaleb up and pats the edge of the bed for him to come sit next to her. Ulla has a tear welling up in her eye.

KALEB
What's wrong, mommy?
ULLA
I just needed to hold you. Mommy saw some scary things tonight. I was just thinking about other kids' mommies and how hard things would be ...
KALEB
It's okay. Don't cry.
ULLA
(wiping her eyes)
Promise me you will never use a needle to do drugs. You have to promise me.

KALEB
Drugs?
ULLA
Just promise Mommy, ok?

She grabs little Kaleb and just hugs him tightly. They sit in that tearful embrace while the voice over plays.

KODY (V.O.)
I may not have known exactly what she was talking about at the time, but for some reason, the memory of that night was burned into my psyche. I didn't keep all my promises I made to my mother, but that one I did.
CUT TO:

## 14    P2-7A: INT. KALEB'S LIVING ROOM - AFTERNOON

Young Kaleb, 8, is sitting on the couch looking out the window with his chunky grey tabby-cat lounging on the back of the couch looking out the window, too.

ELEONORE
(thick German accent)
I don't think he's coming, Kaleb. He does this all the time, I just don't want you to keep getting your hopes up, ok?

KALEB

But, but... He promised this time we would go get Power Rangers stuff at Toys R Us! He promised.

ELEONORE

Okay, Kaleb. I'm going to make dinner now, just in case.

CUT TO:


15    P2-7B: EXT. KALEB'S CHILDHOOD
        HOME - EARLY EVENING

Kaleb sits on the curb with his head in his hands. He hears a car and sees headlights and gets excited. He stands up off the curb only to see the car drive by. He finally gives up and slowly saunters back to the room, not even turning his head when his mother's car pulls into the driveway. He knew the sound of her car. He was broken again and again by his father this way.

CUT TO:


16    P2-8A: INT. KALEB'S CHILDHOOD
        HOME - DAY

Ulla is seen bringing one of her old nurse uniforms (a white dress with a collar) from her room into Kaleb's room. We see Kaleb, 12, brushing a cheap drugstore blonde wig as *Ace of Base's 'ALL THAT SHE WANTS'* plays on his boombox.


ULLA

Are you absolutely sure you want to go dressed like this? I don't want you to get your feelings hurt if some of the other kids say stuff.

KALEB

Mom, I'm not a little kid anymore.

I want to be a nurse, like you. Ok?

ULLA

Okay, Kaleb. Here, you can use some of my favorite lipstick for tonight.

CUT TO:


17    P2-8B: EXT. STREET TO KALEB'S FATHER'S HOUSE - NIGHT

It's Halloween night and Kaleb is dressed up like a female nurse. Lots of kids and their parents can be seen trick-or-treating as well. Kaleb feels so confident in his costume and gets candy from the next-door neighbor of his Father's house. He and Ulla make their way to his Father's door and knock.

CUT TO:


18    P2-8C: INT. KALEB'S FATHER'S HOUSE - NIGHT

Kaleb plays with his step-siblings, who are all dressed in gender-matching costumes. His two older step-brothers are superheroes, and his younger step-sister is a princess. Through the doorway to the kitchen, we see Kaleb's dad talking loudly to Ulla.

KALEB'S FATHER

What the hell, Ulla? No son of mine is going to be seen dressed like that. It's not right... it's disgusting.

ULLA

(pointing to the kids)

Keep your voice down. They can hear you.

(shaking her head)

You don't get to decide what he wears or who he wants to be. You lost that right a long time ago.

KALEB'S FATHER

This is your fault, you know that. If you had a man in your life and didn't let him play with dolls - he wouldn't be like this.

ULLA

You know what? Go Fuck yourself. We're leaving.

Ulla bursts through the door and grabs Kaleb by the hand and pulls him to the door. The kids all look shocked. Kaleb starts to cry.

KALEB'S FATHER

And now he's crying... you see that Ulla... you're raising a baby.

Ulla flips him off and slams the door as she and Kaleb exit.

CUT TO:


19     P2-9: INT. JUNIOR HIGH SCHOOL
                  HALLWAY

Kaleb is now a Junior High aged boy, kind of chunky,

with glasses and hair parted down the middle. Kids are snickering and pointing at him. You can see one of the kids saying "gay." OVER THIS;

KODY (V.O.)
The kids weren't very nice to me. The hallways were a place of torture for a young, chunky, nerdy, and flamboyant little boy.

Kaleb walks out of a classroom into the hall where another boy from his class runs by and swipes his glasses off his face.

ANNOYING BOY
Come catch me if you can four-eyes!

The annoying boy runs down the hallway and Kaleb chases him - dropping his backpack and trapper keeper where he was standing. The CAMERA BLURS in Kaleb's POV as he runs, and when he finally makes it up to the annoying boy, the CAMERA goes back into focus at the exact moment Kaleb barrels into the annoying boy and pushes him down. This was one of the rare moments where young Kaleb turned his anger into physicality. He lands on the annoying boy and starts to slap him, kids start to circle, and the two boys sort of wrestle on the floor of the hallway.

KALEB
Give them back, you... you jerk.

ANNOYING BOY
Get off me, you fat-ass nerd.
KALEB
(pulling the glasses from the annoying boy's hand)
Go Fuck Yourself!

A teacher steps in and pulls them apart. We see the teacher talking to Kaleb as if it was his fault and the annoying kid can be seen behind them making faces as Kaleb gets in trouble.

Kaleb flips off the boy behind his back as he is guided down the hallway.
CUT TO:


20    P2-10: EXT. KALEB'S FATHER'S HOUSE
- MIDDAY

We see Kaleb, 13, and his stepmother and step-siblings watching his father being arrested. Kaleb watches in the yard of his father's home as his father (a tall, handsome, black-haired bear of a man) is arrested and put into a police car. We see Kaleb run up to his father standing near the car.

KALEB'S FATHER
I'm sorry I wasn't a better father to you, Kaleb. One day I will see you again...
KODY (V.O.)
My father had come and gone in my life and one day... he was gone for good.

The police take Kaleb's father and place him into the back seat of the squad car - pushing his head under the door frame like we had seen in so many movies before - but this was real life. As the car starts to pull away, Kaleb runs after the car and cries as he falls to his knees in the middle of the street as the car drives out of view.

CUT TO:


21    P2-11: INT. HIGH SCHOOL GYM - DAY

We see Kaleb, 17, in the high school gym. Kaleb is the only boy trying out for cheerleader at his Texas high school. Half the crowd can be seen booing and the other half cheering. Kaleb can be seen doing all the right moves with the cheerleaders in the cheer section of the tryout but when it comes to the gymnastics part of the audition, there is a bit of nervousness that washes over his face. OVER THIS;


KODY (V.O.)

People said I was a brave young man and I always went for what I wanted. I wasn't afraid to be the first boy to try out for cheerleader at my school... but it didn't help the rumors.


Kaleb walks up to the long mat. He prepares himself for the run and the tricks he will do. Just as he is about to start there is a commotion in the stands.

A pixie-cut red-headed female student soccer player gets out of her seat and runs to the front of the bleachers. She has a rolled-up poster in her hand. When she gets in front of the crowd of students she opens up the poster and reveals the message: **Kaleb's Got Balls!** She runs across the length of the bleachers and students cheer for her bravery in supporting Kaleb. As she makes it to the other end, a teacher grabs her to discipline her - the students cheer again.

Kaleb once again prepares to run. He starts off good with a roundoff but then falls on his back handspring - a silence comes over the crowd, but he gets back up and finishes with a cartwheel. OVER THIS;

KODY (V.O.)

I didn't make the squad. But I did gain a new respect from the kids in my school, I think. I mean, that was the first time anyone but my mom really stood up for me in that way. I was brave that day, and I think it inspired some people to be brave, too.

CUT TO:

22    P2-12: EXT. - COFFEE SHOP - NIGHT

Outside of a local coffee shop where Kaleb works, he closes and locks the door for the night, he walks to his silver Mazda Miata and is approached by three boys around his age.

OVER THIS;

KODY (V.O.)

I didn't really need a job, but my mother wanted me to get a feel for the real world - and I wanted to have my own money. I also wanted to meet new people outside my school.

(MORE)

KODY (V.O.) (CONT'D)

But not all the new people I met had my best interests at heart.


They begin to call him names and attack him.


ATTACKER TEEN 1

Awww, you thought I was really gonna take you on a date, you fucking queer?!


The boys start to circle him - one flicks Kaleb's hair, one is making kissy faces at him, and the other slaps his ass.


ATTACKER TEEN 2

(slapping Kaleb on the ass again)

You like that don't you pussy boy?

ATTACKER TEEN 3

(slapping Kaleb in the groin area)

Probably his gay fantasy - three dudes roughing him up.


The boys are laughing but Kaleb is just frozen -

as they push him and start to punch him. He falls to the ground - he tries to fight back but then one boy slams Kaleb's head into the driver's side door of the Miata while another laughs and scratches the word FAG into the hood of the car. The boys realize Kaleb is no longer conscious and run away. OVER THIS;


KODY (V.O.)
One night I was brutally attacked outside the coffee shop I worked at. It appeared to be a hate crime – a gay bashing - and I barely survived.
CUT TO:


23      P2-13: INT. HOSPITAL ICU ROOM - NIGHT

We see a Kaleb, 17, laying in an ICU bed – tubes helping him breathe – his mother looks scared. His face is bandaged. Nose broken. Bruised eyes and lips. His mother cries, sitting next to his bed, holding his hand, afraid she might lose her only child. We see and hear Kaleb's mother praying over her child's still body.


ULLA
Dear God, Please don't take my son. Don't take my only child. I don't think I could live without him.


She holds her hands so tightly just praying as she watches the tubes help her son breathe. She is always the nurse for other people and their kids... she hasn't been on this side of the situation in this drastic of a fashion before. She is visibly shaken and scared. But then Kaleb's hand twitches and his eye tries to open. OVER THIS;


KODY (V.O.)

But somehow I did survive. Maybe my mother's prayers were answered. Or, maybe, I guess, the Universe just had big plans for this kid - and it wasn't going to let me die yet.

CUT TO:


24    P2-14A: INT. HOSPITAL CANCER WARD
– DAY

We see Kaleb, 17, with his mother, she has lost all her hair and is trying to be strong. His mother, ULLA, in a hospital bed, her hair is gone, she smiles weakly as Kaleb holds her hand. His Grandmother looks on with tears in her eyes. OVER THIS;


KODY (V.O.)

My mother wasn't so lucky. Soon after I healed, she went in for chemo and a bone marrow transplant which cured her leukemia...

CUT TO:

## 25    P2-14B: INT. HOSPITAL CANCER WARD – NIGHT

Weeks later, Kaleb - now 20 days after turning 18 - is in the room and his mother looks like he did in the ICU scene – tubes coming out of her nose and mouth, cords wrapped around the bed, unconscious. OVER THIS;

KALEB (V.O.)
...but due to a post-operative infection, she didn't make it.

A nurse flips the switch on the machine helping Ulla breathe and she passes away, Kaleb says a prayer holding his mother's hand.

KALEB
Dear God, If you want to let my mother live, please let her live. If you need to take her home with you, then please take her home and relieve her suffering. Please tell her I will be okay somehow.

Kaleb consoles his grandmother – staying strong in the moment.
CUT TO:

## 26     P2-14C: INT. HOSPITAL SUPPLY CLOSET - NIGHT

Kaleb is in a supply closet sitting and crying on the floor, his arms wrapped around his knees. OVER THIS;

KODY (V.O.) We lost her due to a post-op infection. To say I was devastated would be an understatement. But it made me grow up real fast.
CUT TO:

## 27     P2-15: INT. LUTHERAN CHURCH - MIDDAY

Ulla lays in an open casket, the morticians tried to do their best to make her look like herself. Her favorite red wig that closely resembled the real hair she lost was situated perfectly but she didn't look much like the vibrant Ulla we had seen in scenes prior. Kaleb, 18, is at the pulpit directly behind the casket and speaks to a full house. Some of Kaleb's high school best friends sit in the front row next to his currently empty seat.

KALEB
...and clearly, she was loved by so many. I thank you all so much for being here. For me... and for her. She was the best mom a kid could ever ask for. She just let me be me.
(a single tear falls down his face)

She loved me unconditionally. She loved her patients and their families. She was an incredibly strong woman and I just hope I can be like her one day.

KALEB (CONT'D)

(looking down at the casket)

I love you, Mom. Thank you for ...

everything.

(he wipes the tear and straightens up - he has to stay strong)

I know she would be so happy that you all came today.

(he nods to the back of the room and the music begins to play)

*Sarah McLachlan's 'ANGEL'* begins to play as we...
FADE TO BLACK.


28    P2-16: MONTAGE OF VARIOUS PHOTOS AND SCRAPBOOKS

We see pictures from Kody's first college scrapbook entitled, "TCU." Stickers and logos can be seen around the photos. "NYC" stickers and writing can be seen around the photos of Carnegie Hall and Sarah Summer's first drag performance in NYC. OVER THIS;

KODY (V.O.)

After I buried my mother and graduated high school, I went to college for a minute – but it wasn't really for me. However, during that time, I met a boy,

I performed at Carnegie Hall, and I made the decision to move to New York City to host my own drag show.
CUT TO:

## 29    P2-17: VIDEO CLIPS (RICKI LAKE CLIP/ KODY ON HOLLYWOOD BLVD)

We see a clip from Kody/Sarah's first television performance on the Ricki Lake show in a Britney Spears outfit (no audio).
OVER THIS;

KODY (V.O.)
I started to gain fame, performing as Britney Spears. I was on the Ricki Lake show, Tyra, and even got asked to audition for a role in Miss Congeniality 2, which I booked.

Real Ricki Lake video clip (audio from clip now plays) and Real Hollywood Blvd videos (audio from clip plays).
More photos of Kody and a photo of Kody's ex-lover, the porn star, appear on the screen as the VO resumes.

KODY (V.O.)
While I was in LA, I fell in love with a porn star and moved to be with him. That relationship lasted about as long as one of his videos. But my relationship with Hollywood lasted a lot longer.

CUT TO:

## 30    P2-18: ANOTHER MONTAGE OF VARIOUS PHOTOS AND VIDEOS

We see images from Kody's Facebook – at the cake shop, delivering the cake to the first legal gay marriage in California, and pictures with Hugh Hefner at the Playboy Mansion.
OVER THIS;

KODY (V.O.)
Then I found what I thought was the perfect job. Managing the most popular celebrity cake shop in LA.

A video from a news segment on the cake shop featuring Kody drunk on the cake shop counter. Then more photos of Kody with celebrities and cakes. OVER THIS;

KALEB (V.O.)(CONT'D)
I mean, with all the sweetness around me, you'd think my life wouldn't have ended up so sour ... but I had a taste for danger, I guess? Or something like that.
CUT TO:

## 31    P2-19: EXT. WEST HOLLYWOOD STREETS - AFTERNOON

Kaleb leaves the cake shop on Santa Monica Blvd

– looking almost the same as he did when revealed initially in the dream sequence – and makes his way up the block to Sunset Blvd and the bar, The State Room, where the story of this series truly begins. The camera walks behind Kaleb as he struts his way up the stretch of street. OVER THIS;

KODY (V.O.)
But, really, it seemed like I had it all. And if I hadn't been drinking and using drugs, my life would have been pretty perfect. But it wasn't. I was holding on to a darkness that I didn't even recognize. Repressed emotions have a way of clawing their way out – one way or another. And my life had become wrapped up in the bar scene – my escape from having to deal with any real emotions. And one bar, in particular, was my favorite... and it was there that I met him, and where this story really begins...

He enters and a beautiful female bartender waves him in.
CUT TO:

## 32   P2-20: INT. SOUNDSTAGE INTERVIEW ROOM - DAY

Kody sits on a soundstage surrounded by lights – the lights are set for recording now - and TV production equipment is out of frame. He speaks from this spot once again.

KODY

Okay, so that's pretty much all the big stuff. Of course, there is some other childhood trauma, but maybe we'll come back to that one of these days. I want this show to really strike a chord with people. I want people to connect... to see themselves in my struggle and hopefully make them feel not so alone with their own issues.

(he flicks his hair dangling in front of his eye out of the way)

Isn't that with this is all about? Telling our story to help or inspire others? Clearly, this story has a happy ending...

(he opens his arms and gives recognition to where he is)

...but, damn, the road to get here was anything but happy.

(turning to look at the TV)

THIS is where my story really gets interesting...

ZOOM BACK INTO TV:

## 33    1-1: INT. STATE ROOM BAR - AFTERNOON

Kaleb is literally dancing into the bar with his head-phones on. NATALIE, a gorgeous light brown-haired bartender, smiles as she sees him come in. Kaleb is dressed in a tight black t-shirt, tight black jeans, black cowboy boots, a top hat, a trench coat (that we recognize from the dream), and one studded black glove. He thinks he is king of the bar and his swagger shows it.

NATALIE
Well, hello, hello lady of the afternoon! What were you listening to?
KALEB
(Playfully)
Hello, bar wench.
Britney Spears, of course. The new album just came out, and I am LIVING for it.

Natalie passes Kaleb a shot (Fireball) and his favorite drink (Whiskey + Diet Coke), and as he downs the shot, a gorgeous, tall, shaggy-haired man, LIAM, walks in behind him and sits at the other end of the bar. The electricity in the room has just sparked and we can tell because Kaleb is now sitting up very straight and looking flirty.
CUT TO:

## 34    1-2: INT. STATE ROOM BAR – LATE AFTERNOON

Kaleb sees Liam ordering a Fireball shot (Kaleb's favorite) and decides to walk over and sit next to the handsome man he has yet to meet. Kaleb orders a Fireball shot as well and they begin to chat.

KALEB

Hey, Nat. I'll take a shot of that, too.

Kaleb looks at Liam and scoots in closer.

KALEB (CONT'D) Fireball, huh? I freakin' love Fireball.

LIAM

Fuck yeah. Hits the spot real good, am I right?

KALEB

Mmhmm. It reminds me of swallowing a whole pack of...

LIAM

... of Big Red gum, right?

Kaleb smiles incredibly big.

KALEB

Yeah. How did you know I was going to say... it was my mom's favorite. It was the only gum she had ever bought.

LIAM

Yeah. It's my favorite, too.

CUT TO:


## 35    1-3: INT. STATE ROOM BAR –
## AFTERNOON INTO NIGHT

A montage of Kaleb and Liam doing shots, smoking cigarettes, touching each other as they laugh, there is a real energy between them.

Kaleb and Liam get very close both emotionally and physically in this montage of bar fun. It is an odd pairing – a straight man and a top-hat-wearing flamboyant guy – but the world around them disappears as they get to know each other better.

CUT TO:


## 36     1-4: INT. STATE ROOM BAR - NIGHT

Kaleb is sitting so close to Liam their legs are touching under the bar - they are old pros at drinking with high tolerances, so they are intoxicated but just enough to be "happy drunk."

NATALIE waves her hand in front of the two to bring them back to reality.

NATALIE
Hello...gentlemen. Last call, ok?
KALEB
Oh. Yeah. Of course. Damn, where did the time go?

The two new friends close their tabs and get up from their seats. They almost don't want to part – but Liam places his hand on Kaleb's lower back as they walk out the door.

LIAM
Should we do this again tomorrow?

Kaleb nods and lets Liam gently guide him out the door with that masculine hand on his back.

CUT TO:

37    1-5: EXT. STATE ROOM BAR – 2:00 AM

Kaleb and Liam shake hands and their hands linger in the grip before they part ways. The energy in the air is palpable as the two say their goodbyes.

KALEB
I had a REALLY good time today.
LIAM
Yeah. Me, too. For sure - me, too.

They look into each other's eyes and finally part. Liam walks in one direction towards Sunset Blvd and Kaleb heads down towards the same street he walked up.
CUT TO:

38    1-6: INT. KALEB'S APARTMENT – 2:20 AM

Kaleb basically floats into his West Hollywood apartment - he is so happy and surprised at how his day turned out.

Kaleb's apartment is in the middle of that street (Hancock Ave.) between Santa Monica Blvd and Sunset Blvd – between his work world and his bar world. He walks into his large, modern-style, one-bedroom apartment and throws his hat and jacket on the couch as he hurries to his bedroom to write in his journal.

He opens to a new page and writes: "Did I just meet THE ONE?"

FADE TO BLACK.

THEN CUT TO:

## 39 1-7A: INT. SOUNDSTAGE INTERVIEW ROOM - DAY

Start on Kody on a couch THEN ZOOM OUT TO A WIDE and REVEAL Ricki Lake as the interviewer sitting across from him. She speaks holding Kody's memoir *Hollywood Heartbreak | New York Dreams* and flipping through the pages:

RICKI

Wait, wait, wait. Is this just a love story? What about all the juicy stuff... from homeless to Harvard ... when does that happen?

KODY

Well, Ricki Lake – I'm so glad you agreed to do this...

(Kody is giddy that she is there)

You were my first TV appearance, and now you're a part of my most important TV appearance – but yes, it is a love story ... just not simply THAT kind of love story. It's about learning to TRULY love yourself, and if I hadn't met 'Liam' and not had my heart broken... we probably wouldn't be here today. I probably wouldn't be here...

*He should be dead after all the drama during his long bout with addiction/alcoholism.*

KODY (CONT'D)
...that's why this part of this story is so important – it's the heartbreak in Heartbreak Dreams. It's the catalyst that changed everything.

Kody grabs a remote and presses fast forward and we see his life flashing before our eyes – ZOOM INTO TV AGAIN -he stops on the night he considered suicide steps away from Liam's house.
FAST FORWARD
CUT TO:


40      1-7B: EXT. HOLLYWOOD HILLS STREET
                - 3 A.M.

We see Kaleb walking down a street [we find out in a later scene this is Liam's street] in the dark, shivering a bit, and stopping when he comes across some broken glass on the ground next to a curb. Kaleb grabs the biggest, sharpest piece of glass and sits on the curb. OVER THIS;


KODY (V.O.)
We COULD skip ahead to the night of my heartbreak, the night I nearly gave up on it all. The night I thought a shattered piece of glass - resembling what I'm sure my heart looked like – would solve all my

problems. But there was a quiet voice inside my head that told me to keep going... I think it was my mother.

Video FAST FORWARDS again.

CUT TO:

41     1-7C: EXT. NYC CITY STREET – BRONX – LATE NIGHT

OPEN ON Kaleb leaving a homeless shelter drunk and high and going to look for crack to share with one of his shelter buddies. He winds up at the projects [city-ran affordable housing complex] in the Bronx, where a muscular African American guy seems to begin to make a drug deal with him. OVER THIS:

KODY (V.O.)

I could skip to the part where I was attacked outside the projects by a crack dealer who did me dirty half a block from the second homeless shelter I stayed at in the Bronx...

DRUG DEALER

You got the money?

KALEB

(slurred and agitated) Of course, I got the money. You think I'm some kinda bitch? A fucking crack whore?

DRUG DEALER What the fuck you say to me, faggot?

The drug dealer attacks and robs Kaleb, leaving him

beaten up – a large gash cut into his chin from falling and hitting the pavement – blood pours profusely out of the wound onto the street, and the crack dealer rushes away, leaving Kaleb scared and alone.

KODY (V.O.)

... and how that one night, that one attack, changed my appearance for the rest of my life.


FAST FORWARD ON TV
CUT TO:


## 42    1-7D: EXT. HARVARD YARD - AFTERNOON

*KODY* walks through the Johnston Gate into Harvard Yard and stands proudly in front of the John Harvard statue as he clutches a pink fuzzy pen and heart-shaped notebook. (*This foreshadows the potential for Kody Christiansen to play himself in later episodes.*) OVER THIS;


KODY (V.O.)

And, I guess, I could skip all the way to the end to my Elle Woods moment in Harvard Yard and tell you how I became an undergraduate student a couple of years into my sobriety ... but then we would miss out on so much of the bad stuff that in its own way was really the good stuff. You know what I mean?

## 43    1-8: INT. SOUNDSTAGE INTERVIEW ROOM - DAY

START ON Kody and Ricki sitting across from each other [TWOSHOT FROM SIDE]. Kody teases Ricki.

KODY

Hell, I could even tell you about the pile of human feces that completely shook my world and changed my life forever... but we gotta save something for the arc of this interview, right?

RICKI

I can't disagree with you there – I know all too well about sweeps and the big reveals. Okay, you've sold me...

(Ricki looks into the camera to her left.)

...when we return, we will go back to Hollywood to find out why this relationship with a Rockstar turned out to be the catalyst that changed Kody's life.

DIRECTOR (O.S.) CUT!

FADE TO BLACK

## ACT TWO

## 44    2-1: INT. SOUNDSTAGE INTERVIEW ROOM - DAY

FADE IN:

START ON Kody and Ricki relaxing briefly – Kody sips from his

Harvard mug and Ricki reads over some note cards.

The DIRECTOR is off-camera, but HIS HAND comes into the frame to countdown before the next segment of the interview begins.

DIRECTOR
(Whispers)
Three, two, one, action.

Ricki looks into the left camera.

RICKI
We are back with Kody Christiansen coming to you from Hollywood, California, where Kody is so bravely sharing his story with us in hopes of inspiring others.
(looks back to Kody still holding a copy of his first memoir)
Before we continue Kody, what was the most difficult part about writing your books?
KODY
Well, Ricki, when I was writing the first book and the script for the show we are on [super meta], it was kinda tough going through all the stuff I actually went through again and again... ...envisioning the last moments with my mom, getting attacked, love, addictions ... just having to go back there in my mind was tough. I found different ways to cope - imagining myself as a character in my own story was one of them. It helped some, but it is still hard to think about all of it when I write it again, even with the alias.
RICKI

That makes sense.
(she closes the book and sets it down on the table)
KODY
I may have also given Liam a few more abs than he actually had. That helped. Ha.
(they both chuckle at that comment.)
RICKI
Thank you for asking me to be here with you for this exclusive interview to tell your story... It's really an honor. Now, let's continue. So, what happened next with the Rockstar?
KODY
Well.. the next day...
CUT TO:


## 45    2-2: EXT. STATE ROOM BAR – HOLLYWOOD - AFTERNOON

OPEN ON Kaleb and Liam arrive nearly at the exact same time and give each other a warm "man-hug" (the one-arm kinda thing) at the entrance to the bar.


LIAM
Hey, hey.
KODY
Hey, hey to you, too.
LIAM
Nice boots. Let's get a fucking drink.
CUT TO:

## 46    2-3: INT. STATE ROOM BAR - HOLLYWOOD - AFTERNOON

Kaleb and Liam cozy up to the bar, NATALIE has two shots of Fireball waiting for them. They clink shot glasses, and after gulping it down, Liam puts his arm around Kaleb and points to the TV above them. Kaleb looks at Liam's hand as it is now so close to his face and just smiles. This is too good to be true.

LIAM
So, Kaleb. You a big fan of sports?
KALEB
Well, I'm not opposed to watching hot men in tight uniforms play with balls.
LIAM
(nearly spitting out his drink)
That's funny. You're funny. I like it.
(he gets up off his barstool)
I'll be right back.

This is a trend Kaleb noticed happening a few times the day before but didn't say anything. Did Liam have a small bladder or was something else going on?

## 47    2-4: INT. STATE ROOM BAR – HOLLYWOOD - AFTERNOON

Kaleb sips his drinks and looks at his phone - patiently waiting for Liam to return to the bar. A hand touches Kaleb on the shoulder, surprising him, and he turns to see a RANDOM BAR GUY wearing glasses, nearly salivating.

RANDOM BAR GUY
Hey, hey... can I get an autograph?
Kaleb gives the guy a perplexed look.
KALEB
Umm.. sure, I'll give you my autograph. Did you see me on Ricki Lake a few years ago or something? Or on the news - the cake shop thing?
RANDOM BAR GUY
No...no. Your friend! That's Liam Sparks! Do you think I could get his autograph?
KALEB
What are you talking about, man? Who is Liam Sparks? Maybe you have him confused with some-one else.
RANDOM BAR GUY
(slurred)
No, no, no, no... that's him. You know the song... la, la, la, hmmm... I tried so hard ...
(slur turns into a murmur and he stumbles back to his seat)

Kaleb pulls his laptop out of his bag (he sometimes does work for the cake shop at the bar) and Googles Liam Sparks. Oh wow. Liam Sparks was the frontman of a big rock band from the late 90s/early 2000s, and

Kaleb knew some of the songs by heart. Why didn't Liam tell him this?

Kaleb is visibly confused.

CUT TO:

## 48    2-5: INT. STATE ROOM BAR – AFTERNOON

At the bar Kaleb is a bit hurt - another man in his life that was lying to him. How could his new friend keep this info from him? Liam returns wiping his nose and sniffling a bit.

KALEB

Liam Sparks, huh? What the hell? You weren't gonna tell me you were a freakin' Grammy winner?

LIAM

Kaleb, you were the first person in years who didn't automatically know who I was.

And? Should I be like bowing at your feet or asking you to sign my ass or something?

LIAM

No. No, that's not it. You liked me for me, Kaleb. You just fucking liked me for me - not who I am, who I was - or what I can give you or do for you. You were you and I was just me. And that was enough for me.

KALEB

(nearly tearing up)

Damn.

Kaleb finds this notion endearing and decides to tell him about Sarah Summers.

KALEB (CONT'D)
Well, okay. So, now that I know who you are... let me show you who I am.

Kaleb shows Liam some photos and videos of him as Sarah on his computer. Liam's jaw quite literally drops a bit. He takes a deep breath.

LIAM
Fuck. You make a beautiful woman and a good-looking guy. How is that fair to anyone? Ha.
*Kaleb puts his hand to his heart. Did the man of his dreams just say he was beautiful in either gender?*
KALEB
(nervous giggle)
I don't make the rules, stud.
LIAM
Natalie! Two more shots of Fireball for me and the fucking undercover hottie over here.
NATALIE
No prob.

Liam and Kaleb just kind of sit and stare at each other for a moment while Natalie prepares the drinks. They had just revealed another side to each other and the connection grew.

Natalie brings over the shots and Kaleb and Liam's

hands touch as they reach for the same shot glass. They feel the spark and then laugh as they throw back the shots.

LIAM
(pointing to the cigar lounge directly behind them)
Why don't we go get a little more comfortable?

## 49    2-6: INT. STATE ROOM CIGAR LOUNGE – EARLY EVENING

Now, in the corner of the "Backroom" of the State Room Bar (the cigar lounge), sitting in brown leather seats, the two are getting even closer. CAMERA PANS IN on Liam already mid-sentence.

LIAM
...and she was like, "oh, fuck baby! You're so big - slap me with it."
(Liam takes a swig of his whisky)
I love that kinda shit.
KALEB
Well, come on - who wouldn't be all over that... especially when you are on tour? I heard groupies can be crazy.
LIAM
(putting his hand on Kaleb's knee)
You have no idea, K. Like I've fucked some really crazy chicks over the years - like insane crazy, not just crazy in the sack.

KALEB
(grabs Liam's hand - playfully says)
Oh wow. I'm so, so sorry, Mister Rockstar - that must have been so hard for you.
LIAM
It ain't easy being sleazy, baby!
KALEB
(literally SMH - slaps his own hand to his forehead)
Oh my god. Ha. You're a mess. But I'm here for it.


Liam pats Kaleb's knee with his hand and ends with a bit of a squeeze. Kaleb sort of flinches with excitement and catches a little tickle from it, too.

Liam winks and once again gets up to use the bathroom, but this time Kaleb follows him to quell his suspicions.
CUT TO:


## 50    2-7 INT. STATE ROOM BATHROOM - EARLY EVENING

The bathroom door is unlocked, and Liam is waiting for Kaleb. *'CRUSH' by Jennifer Paige* begins to play.


LIAM
I knew you'd be coming.


Kaleb approaches Liam – their bodies are so close they could have kissed. Liam turns Kaleb towards the mirror and, from behind him, pulls a key up to Kaleb's nose with white powder on the end.

LIAM (CONT'D)
You ready for this?

Kaleb nods, knowing if he spoke a word or exhaled, the powder would fall off the key.

SLOW MOTION. The song *'CRUSH'* remixes into a slowed-down sexier version as Kaleb feels safe with Liam and snorts the cocaine. The rush goes to his head and a warm RED LIGHT appears as Kaleb's hands drop and rest on Liam's thighs standing behind him.
FADE TO BLACK.

## 51    2-8: INT. STATE ROOM BATHROOM – EARLY EVENING

*'BACK TO LIFE' by Soul II Soul* is playing on the bar speakers and can be heard softly through the bathroom door. The red glow from the end of the previous scene is still visible as this scene starts where the last one ended. Liam snorts a key of cocaine standing behind Kaleb – body to body – and they experience this moment together. Liam turns Kaleb around to look into his eyes. Liam's emerald green and Kaleb's sky blue – the moment is intense.

LIAM

Kaleb, do you want to suck my dick?
KALEB
(shocked and nervous)
Umm... what?
*Kaleb definitely heard him.*
CUT TO:
Kaleb envisions it for a moment. To the audience, it looks like Kaleb is actually about to go through with it - getting on his knees and looking up and unbuttoning and unzipping Liam's pants.
CUT BACK TO:
The moment before. Real time. The red aura is gone – Kaleb plays it off as a joke – afraid to ruin the blossoming relationship if he gives into his carnal desires.

KALEB (CONT'D)
Hey, stop playing around. It isn't very nice to tease a boy, ya know?

Kaleb goes to exit the bathroom; Liam stops him by pushing one hand against the door and placing the other on Kaleb's hand that is resting on the doorknob, then turning him around.

LIAM
I'm not fucking around here, K. I want you to suck my dick. Don't you want to?
KALEB

I'm ... uh ... too fucking high for this right now Liam. Come on.

Kaleb resists again because he wants to see where this whole thing goes and giving in too soon could ruin it all. Kaleb walks out of the bathroom leaving Liam in the doorway confused – he has probably never been told no before.


ACT THREE


52    3-1 INT. CAKE SHOP - WEST HOLLYWOOD - LATE MORNING – TWO WEEKS LATER

*OPEN WITH MONTAGE:* Kaleb is answering phones and helping customers as they walk in. He looks annoyed as he puts a cupcake tray into the oven. He does some graphic work on the computer and walks out to the back for a smoke break.

It is clear he would rather be at the bar but tries to maintain a faux smile throughout the different shots in the montage. We finally settle on Kaleb at the front desk as a customer is walking out the door after placing an order.

KALEB
(fake smile)
Thank you! See you in two weeks.

Then the phone rings. He rolls his eyes. The work is so monotonous.

KALEB (CONT'D)

(on the phone)

Hello - Hollywood Cakes. How can I help you? Mhmm.. a bridal shower cake? Like one of the penis cakes, correct?

(he grabs a pen and an order pad - this call is at least fun)

Mhmm. So, did you want the erect penis with the icing coming out of the top to look like... you know... or the laying down cut-out penis-type cake?

(he smiles to himself as the client is talking)

Ahh, yes. Okay - erect penis with icing "stuff" coming out the top. Now, the important question: What color skin tone?

(he writes down the answer)

Oh, yeah, no problem. And that is for when?

Kaleb continues to take the order, and we PAN OUT to see the cake shop getting busier, but then we PAN IN to the Wizard of Oz clock on the pink wall, and it shows it is nearly noon. Kaleb realizes he has to go meet Liam soon.

KALEB (CONT'D)

Great. Big dick for the 29th at 2 pm. Got it. Thanks.

Kaleb hangs up the phone quickly and then throws

off his apron as he puts the order form in a box below the register.

## 53 3-1B INT. CAKE SHOP - WEST HOLLYWOOD - LATE MORNING

Kaleb is just about to walk out the front door when the owner

TIM (55, a grey-haired man with a joyful demeanor who is Kaleb's boss and has basically taken on the role of parental figure) stops him.

TIM

Kaleb - where are you going? There is so much work to do. You know we are short-staffed today.

KALEB

(fake smile and fibbing)

It's lunchtime. I ... uh ... promised I would meet a potential client for lunch. This could be a big deal for the shop. It's important that I go.

TIM

(with a disappointed look)

Okay, Kaleb... but I expect you back in an hour. There is lots of work left to do.

They both knew Kaleb wouldn't be back that day. This was a pattern that had begun to be more frequent after Kaleb met Liam. Tim had seen Kaleb at his best but also knew that he had issues with alcohol and suspected that there was someone new in Kaleb's life who might be a bad influence, but let Kaleb go that day, knowing he would have to pick up the slack. His fatherly role in Kaleb's life took on many forms and this was one.

## 54     3-2: EXT. STATE ROOM - CIGAR LOUNGE – AFTERNOON

The instrumental track to *'JOLENE' by Dolly Parton* plays as Kaleb walks up the same street and passes by the window to the Cigar Lounge where he sees Liam talking to a very pretty young woman with dark hair. Liam doesn't notice Kaleb at first. Was Liam flirting with that girl? Kaleb gets suspicious and looks through the window assessing the situation. A look of jealousy can be seen on Kaleb's face, but before the frown freezes, Liam notices him, and the frown turns into a big smile, and Kaleb waves in a flirty manner. No one can know that Kaleb is jealous ... of a woman. Kaleb opens up the camera app on his phone and checks himself to make sure he looks good - he stops and applies some clear lip gloss that is in the pocket of his tight-fitting black jeans.

## 55   3-3: INT. STATE ROOM - CIGAR LOUNGE – AFTERNOON

Despite the interaction with the woman in the previous scene, Kaleb and Liam are closer than ever after two weeks – Kaleb is literally sitting on Liam's lap. Other bar patrons, including the woman Liam was seen talking to, give them odd looks occasionally and the bar staff has begun to call them "husband and wife" when they deliver drinks. NATALIE drops off two drinks at the table.

NATALIE
For Mr. and Mrs. Sparks

*Liam didn't seem to care what people thought, and this afternoon, Liam decided to pop a question.*

LIAM
(shifting in his chair so Kaleb faces him)
Hey, do you want to come see my house in the hills tomorrow?
KALEB
(playfully stroking Liam's hair)
Are you sure you can handle being alone with me, Mr. Sparks?
LIAM
(eases Kaleb off of his lap and into the seat next to him)
We'll see.

## 56    3-4: INT. KALEB'S APARTMENT –
### EARLY EVENING

Kaleb invites his friend Lacy to come over and help him prepare for the evening. Lacy is basically his sister

– they look like twins, they are the same age, they are both actors, and they have been friends for many years. Lacy is the first person in his circle he tells about the new "bromance" with Liam. She is skeptical but as a good friend is there to support.


KALEB

Oh my god, come in, come in.

LACY

(being herded into the apartment quickly)

You called like it was an emergency. What's up?

KALEB

What's up? What is up?! Fucking Liam if I'm extra lucky.

(making a graphic penis gesture with his hands)

LACY

Damn, bitch. You STILL haven't messed around with him? Maybe tonight is the night. Is that what you are gonna wear though?


Kaleb second-guesses his outfit, and they walk to his closet and start digging to find the sexiest rock-star-seducing outfit.

CUT TO:


57    3-5: INT. LACY'S FOUR-DOOR SEDAN - CAR RIDE – EVENING

Kaleb and Lacy drive up into the Hollywood hills

in her four-door silver sedan. Kaleb primps nervously in the mirror.

KALEB
(applying a bit of clear lip gloss)
Is it strange that I feel so incredibly connected to him - but I've only known him for like two weeks? I've only had this feeling with three other guys in my entire life.
LACY
Emotional slut!
(she flips her hair in jest)
I'm kidding. No, I feel you. Wait - three guys? I think I know one of them, right?
KALEB
I mean there was my first college love, Tristan. My first unconditional love, Shane. And that first porn star...
(he hits the dashboard with his hands three times)
That's it -- the big white one with the stairs. Holy shit.

They arrive at Liam's big mansion on the hill and the juxtaposition of Lacy's sedan next to Liam's black vintage '87 Corvette when they park in his driveway is quite noticeable. They have entered the world of the upper echelon now.
CUT TO:

58    3-6 EXT. LIAM'S MANSION - DOORWAY
- EVENING

Liam greets them at the door in a black tank top
and black skinny jeans and gives Kaleb a hug and
shakes Lacy's hand.


LIAM
(waving them in - placing his hand on Kaleb's lower
back as he guides him through the door)
Welcome to my world. Let me give you a little tour.
CUT TO:


59     3-7 INT. LIAM'S MANSION - LIVING
ROOM/BEDROOM/BATHROOM - EVENING

His mansion looks very similar in decorations in
the dream sequence from the opening of the show -
very rock and roll and lots of gold records on the walls.
He shows them around the house and when they get
to the bathroom with the huge walk-in shower:


LIAM
This is probably my favorite fucking part of the
whole damn house. There have definitely been some
wild nights in this shower.
KALEB
(his eyes open wide and he starts to hear the water
that is not there)

Oh, I can imagine...

CUT TO:

Kaleb imagines him and Liam showering together - the steam rising all around them. Liam kisses Kaleb's neck and continues kissing down to his shoulder.

CUT BACK TO:

Real-time - Liam puts his arm on Kaleb's shoulder and motions that Lacy has already moved on to the next stop on the grand tour.

LIAM
Let's keep going.
CUT TO:


## 60    3-8 INT. LIAM'S MANSION - LIVING ROOM - EVENING

They end up in the living room and talk for a minute – Lacy hounding Liam on how they met and what he sees for himself in the future.

LACY
So, you're bar buddies? Hmm. So, what's next?
KALEB
(with a don't-go-there look)
Umm... Lace...
LACY
What's next for your career, Liam?
(pointing to the music awards behind them)

Big plans?

LIAM

Oh, fuck yeah. I'm tryin' to find a new band - the old guys ... well let's just say that isn't gonna happen. Some fucked up shit went down after our last record, so fuck them. Fresh fuckin' start, I say.

KALEB

(looking at Lacy and then glancing at her pink watch)

Hey, didn't you have to go pre...

LACY

...prepare for that audition. Yes.

You're so right, I totally spaced. Big, big audition tomorrow - pilates slash yoga workout something-a-rather. New LA fad, of course. Okay, bye.

Kaleb nods for her to go with a thankful wink and Lacey makes her way to the door and lets herself out. Finally, it is just Liam and Kaleb alone.

CUT TO:


## 61    3-9A: INT. LIAM'S LIVING ROOM – LATE EVENING

Liam walks back into the living room from the kitchen holding two drinks – a whiskey + diet coke for Kaleb and a beer for himself. Liam picks up his acoustic guitar and sits close to Kaleb.

LIAM

I'm working on my comeback album. It's gonna be the fucking comeback of the century!
(touching Kaleb's thigh)
I think you could help me with it.

CONTINUE TO:
*This is a fantasy, but the audience initially believes it is really happening.*

KALEB
Just let me know what you need me to do, Liam.
LIAM
I need you to kiss me right now.

Liam lets his hand slide from Kaleb's thigh up to his neck. He pulls Kaleb into him forcefully, establishing his dominance, but when he kisses Kaleb, it is sweet and soft.

LIAM (CONT'D)
Wow. This is the first time I ever kissed a ... not a girl. Fuck.

Kaleb puts Liam's guitar on the floor then straddles him and pulls his head back towards the arm of the couch and begins to kiss Liam's neck all the way up to a passionate kiss - showing he can be dominant too.
QUICK CUT:
Back to the same position as before the fantasy -

Liam is holding his guitar and one hand on Kaleb's thigh. Kaleb places his hand on Liam's hand.

KALEB
Of course. I would do anything for you.
(biting his lip knowing that was too much, too soon)
I would HELP you with anything to get your career back...
LIAM
I know you would, K. I feel it. I want to sing a song for you.

Liam begins to strum the chords. The familiar Elton John tune, 'Rocket Man,' begins to escape his mouth, and with his raspy rocker voice, it is so sexy and soulful at the same time.

LIAM (CONT'D)
(sung)
I packed my bags last night, preflight. Zero-hour, nine a.m., and I'm gonna be high as a kite by then...

*Kaleb is in love. Maybe Liam is feeling something he has never felt for a guy before. Kaleb joins in after the first chorus and the harmony is magical.*

LIAM AND KALEB
(sung)
And I think it's gonna be a long, long time 'til touchdown brings me 'round again to find I'm not the

man they think I am at home - oh, no, no, no - I'm a rocket man...

FADE TO BLACK.


## ACT FOUR


## 62    4-1: LIAM'S MANSION – LIVING ROOM - EARLY MORNING

The two stay up all night singing, and remnants of cocaine, empty beer bottles, and freshly written lyric ideas are scattered across the table. The sun rises through the sheer black window treatment – the two had been in a dream state partying and singing and sitting oh so close all night. Kaleb looks at his iPhone and realizes it is time to leave.

KALEB
Shit! The 9 to 5 is calling my name. I gotta jet.
LIAM
Fuck work.
KALEB
I wish. Have you seen my boots?
LIAM
Here, ba..
(he hesitates)
K. Here they are.

Once Kaleb is ready, Liam walks him to the door, gives him a tight hug, and whispers in Kaleb's ear.

LIAM (CONT'D)
We should do this again soon.

Kaleb melts and decides to walk down the hill to reenergize with the sun and try to shake himself into a presentable – sober-looking – person before work.
CUT TO:


## 63  4-2: EXT. SUNSET BLVD – EARLY MORNING (VISIONS OF THE FUTURE)

Feeling good after an amazing night with Liam, Kaleb nearly skips down the hill (Sunset Plaza Drive) but, at the same time, is trying to shake off the booze and cocaine so he can be somewhat presentable for work. When he reaches the cross-section between the hill and Sunset Blvd, he rounds the corner to see a homeless man sleeping in a business doorway. Kaleb looks at the guy with pity and leaves a $20 bill.

KALEB
(whispering to himself)
Damn.
(laying down the bill whispering as if he is talking to the sleeping man)
Here you go. How could you let this happen?

FADE OUT:

## 64    4-3 EXT. DIRTY NEW YORK CITY ALLEYWAY – EARLY MORNING

*A white vignette filter is visible over the edges of the following scenes - alerting the audience that these are future happenings.*

Kaleb in the alley way from the opening scene falling into the trash bag pile.

CUT TO:

## 65    4-4 INT. STATE ROOM BATHROOM - NIGHT

Kaleb and Liam are about to snort crystal meth.

LIAM
Wait this is all he had?
KALEB
Yeah, sold out of the kitty. C'mon, Liam - just try it with me. He said it is just a little stronger than coke.
LIAM
Okay... crush it up good, baby.

Kaleb crushes the crystal meth on the top of the toilet tank. Liam rolls up a hundred-dollar bill, and they take turns snorting the substance. Liam looks at Kaleb and pulls him in close - he starts rubbing his shoulders - this high is a different feeling than cocaine. The sexual tension is palpable.

CUT TO:


66      4-5 INT. RAINBOW BAR AND GRILL
                STAGE - NIGHT

Kaleb singing *'CREEP' by Radiohead* at the Rainbow on Sunset Blvd. The upstairs wooden stage that has seen the boots of many famous rockstars over the years is now the place where Kaleb is vulnerable and sharing his soul through song. We see an empty table with a reserved sign among the packed bar - Liam didn't show.

KALEB
(sung)
When you were here before... couldn't look you in the eye. You're just like an angel, your skin makes me cry. You float like a feather in a beautiful world.
(the smoke from the stage rushes under his legs)
KALEB (CONT'D)
(sung)
I wish I was special - you're so fucking special. But I'm a creep, I'm a weirdo, what the hell am I doing here? I don't belong here. I don't care if it hurts...

CUT TO:

## 67    4-6 INT. KALEB'S LIVING ROOM - WEST HOLLYWOOD - AFTERNOON

The song *'CREEP' by Radiohead* plays quietly behind the next *few scenes continuing where Kaleb left off in the last scene.*

We see Kaleb on his living room floor, he is visibly shaken. Next to him is a crystal meth pipe that has been used heavily and a nearly empty bag of crystals. In front of him is an open letter - it is from his father in prison. On the envelope, Kaleb has written Chaplain Grey 917-555-5465.


KALEB

Okay, Chaplain Grey - I understand. Thank you for letting me talk to him. I know you don't do this for many people.

CHAPLAIN GREY

You're welcome, Kaleb. Here he is.

KALEB'S FATHER

Hello, number one son.

KALEB

Hi, dad.

KALEB'S FATHER

So, I know the chaplain told you a little bit about the situation ... they didn't catch it soon enough, son. It doesn't look like I'll be getting out of here.

KALEB

Yeah... I guess not.

KALEB'S FATHER

Kaleb, you know I love you. I've been in here so long - but you never left my mind. I was hoping I'd get to see you again one day... I just want you to know I'm sorry for everything... I'm sorry, son.
KALEB
(tears start to stream down his face)
I know, Dad. I know. I forgive you.
CUT TO:


# 68  4-7 EXT. KALEB'S APARTMENT FRONT DOOR - NIGHT

"Eviction" sign on Kaleb's Hollywood apartment door. Kaleb walks up to the sign and tears it down.

KALEB
(banging fists on the door and screaming)
God Damnit!
CUT TO:


# 69  4-8 EXT. LIAM'S HOUSE - HOLLYWOOD HILLS - LATE NIGHT

Kaleb is slightly intoxicated and standing at Liam's door. He came to ask Liam if he could stay the night with him. He knocks multiple times and no one answers. He turns to leave, but Liam finally opens the door.

KALEB

Liam.
LIAM
Kaleb.
KALEB
Liam, I need to...
LIAM
(cutting Kaleb off)
No, dude. Just no. You can't stay here tonight.
KALEB
What? What did you just call me? And why the fuck not?

As Kaleb begins to completely lose his cool, a big-breasted, good-looking blonde woman walks up behind Liam - she looks like the cisgendered version of Sarah Summers. ANNA LYNN (30, gorgeous blonde who looks strikingly like Kaleb when he is dressed as Sarah Summers) places her hand on Liam's shoulder and motions for him to come back inside.

Kaleb knows her - they were good friends - he is hurt and it is written all over his face.

KALEB (CONT'D)
So... this is how it's gonna be, huh? Just let me stay in one of the empty rooms.
LIAM
You can't stay here tonight, DUDE.

Liam slams the door in Kaleb's face. He had NEVER before called Kaleb ... dude. Kaleb saw right through the facade Liam was putting on for Anna Lynn. Kaleb breaks down in front of the door. He falls to his knees and cries. The love of his life chose a carbon copy cisgendered version of his alter ego. This is the turning point for Kaleb.

CUT TO:

## 70   4-9 EXT./INT. NEW YORK CITY HOMELESS SHELTER - MANHATTAN - AFTERNOON

Kaleb walking into his first homeless shelter looking haggard with only his messenger bag and wearing the same outfit he wore when he sung at the Rainbow - the one outfit he brought to New York. A militarylooking African-American woman sits at the front desk behind the glass - she eyes Kaleb suspiciously.

SELMA
Yo! You checkin' in?
KALEB
Uh, yes, ma'am.
SELMA
Aight. You in room 212. Here's the key. You lose this - you gotta pay for another. There ain't no curfew here - but you can't bring nobody in, you understand?
KALEB
Ok.
SELMA

You gonna meet your case manager in the morning so don't be late.

(she pauses to catch her breath)

OH! And room check is at 9 am - every morning - we gotta make sure you ain't dead. We had people die up in here before.

KALEB

(under his breath)

Shit.


Kaleb takes the key and a piece of paper from the security guard and walks down the hospital-like hall towards an elevator. There is a ring of dirt along the baseboards of the hallway and a faint odor of urine wafting from the stairwell to the right of the elevator. Kaleb looks to the left of the elevator call button to see a bin that looks like a trashcan but there is a sign that reads: **USED NEEDLE DEPOSIT**. Kaleb, for a moment, thinks of his mother on the bed when he was a child.

CUT TO:


## 71    4-9B: FLASHBACK TO SCENE P2-6

ULLA

(wiping her eyes)

Promise me you will never use a needle to do drugs. You have to promise me.

CUT TO:

## 72    4-9C INT. NEW YORK CITY HOMELESS SHELTER - MANHATTAN - AFTERNOON

Kaleb presses the number 2 button and lets out a huge sigh as he waits for the doors to open. After he steps in we see him turn to face the camera and hang his head as the doors close.

CUT TO:


## 73    4-10 INT. SMALL HOMELESS SHELTER SINGLE ROOM - NYC - NIGHT

Kaleb is in a small single-room occupancy shelter room - the TV is on, and we see an evangelical (It was Mike Murdock that night) giving one of those late-night sermons. Kaleb, who had been out for Gay Pride, is dealing with another alcoholic blackout. We see rainbow beads and Pride giveaways scattered on the ground. Next to Kaleb's bed is a plastic grocery bag.

Kaleb picks it up and vomits - his eyes roll back in his head. He collapses on the bed, only to snap back up moments later to barf again. He is really sick. OVER THIS;


EVANGELICAL ON TV

To find your Universal Assignment, your Divine Path, you have to let go of the demons that you have brought upon yourself. Take a look at your life - is this the path that God has laid out for you? We often wonder why bad things happen to us - "Why me, God?" -

we ask out loud. The answer is simple. God is not letting these bad things happen to you because he hates you. No! God is trying to get you back on the path HE has laid out for you. Number five on this list says, "If you rebel against your Divine Assignment then God may permit painful experiences to correct you."
CUT TO:


## 74  4-11 INT. SMALL HOMELESS SHELTER SINGLE ROOM - NYC - MORNING

Kaleb is in the same room and same bed as the prior scene, but he is now writhing in pain, experiencing intense withdrawals. He is sweating, he is shaking, he is crying. He pulls another plastic grocery bag out from under his bed to vomit in because the others are full. He is a mess - but he is determined to beat these addictions - alone. OVER THIS;


EVANGELICAL (V.O.) Your Divine Assignment will require seasons of preparation. The greater the assignment, the longer the more difficult the training will be. You are exactly where the Universe has divinely placed you - at exactly the time the Universe has placed you. Here you have no rivals. The price of your future is your life.


*White vignette over the scenes and the song 'CREEP' by Radiohead end with scene 4-11 as we...*
FADE TO BLACK.

## 75    4-12: INT. SOUNDSTAGE INTERVIEW ROOM - EARLY EVENING

Kody is back on the couch on the soundstage as we pull out from the TV and back to the interview shot with Ricki.

RICKI

Oh, wow. There is just so much to unpack, Kody. You really have lived a crazy life – multiple different lives, really. I can't wait to see what happens next. Of course, I have read your books, but it is just so much more interesting to hear from you directly.

(Ricki looks into the camera to her left)

RICKI (CONT'D)

Okay, viewers, see you next time on Life Story: Kody Christiansen

DIRECTOR (O.S.)

CUT! Check the gates. Great job. That's a wrap. See you all tomorrow.

Kody and Ricki are relaxed once again, the crew starts to pack up.

RICKI

What a day!

(to a crew member - sweetly but powerfully)

Can I get a diet coke... please.

(back to Kody)

I think this interview is going to be so good for both of us. My comeback - your breakout.

(she pauses to bask in the moment)

Did you ever think your life would have ended up like this?

KODY

Honestly, no. I mean, I guess, you never quite know how your life will turn out. You can make all the plans in the world, but if those aren't the world's plans for you – then you better learn to evolve really quick.

RICKI

We don't know our own strengths until we are tested.

KODY

Exactly, Ricki. And, God Damn, was I tested. But you know what's crazy? Even after all of it, I feel like this, right now, is just the beginning...


FADE TO BLACK.

END OF EPISODE

# Acknowledgements

In the last couple of books, I think I have thanked just about everyone in my life who has truly stood by me through thick and thin. Those people, *my water*, will always have my love and gratitude. A few people, like the two I dedicated this book to, I have lost along the way, but the Universe has also gifted me with so many amazing new friends and family since the publication of my last book.

Tom: I have to thank you in every book because you have truly been my family for nearly half of my life. Seeing you at my Harvard graduation with pride in your eyes was a beautiful moment for me. We've been through so much together, and I thank the Universe that you are in my life.

Aimee - *Momma Aimme*: The Universe also knew I needed you and dropped us into each other's lives at just the right time. Love you and thank you for loving me like your own.

Lisa - my sister. So glad we got to experience London and Paris together. Here's to many more years and many more adventures.

Kayla - *Bunny*: Thanks for being an amazing friend for so many years and always having my back. We still need to shoot that short film we wrote!

Danielle: My Harvard Rock! We did so much for our community together. So many hours, so much love, a ton of energy ... and a hearty portion of drama. Thank you for being you.

Georgie: Oh, G. What to say besides xx and woof woof? Love you to pieces and thank you for the love and encouragement over here in the UK. Our Saltburn Christmas and touching Stonehenge with you will be some of my favorite memories for the rest of my life.

Mark - Miles away and still making each other smile. Thanks, PB.

Abbie and Jo - My Gals: The three of us, the McFlurry Mavens, connected forever by those conversations, laughs, tears, and hugs in Perkins 2. Love you both so much,

Adam and Carsyn: OMG. You two and our Merry Crispsmas. Two dear friends that I am so blessed to have in my life. Thank you for the unending support and for laughing at my jokes.

My Queens' family at Cambridge: From the Porter's

Lodge to the Qbar, the Woodville Room, and the Old Hall, you have all made my life so much brighter in so many unique and wonderful ways. Thank you for taking me in.

My Harvard GSAS family: Thank you for every wonderful moment and for the beautiful friendship and mentorship. You all mean the world to me. Lehman Hall, I'll see you soon.

My HES and HESA family: So proud to have stood beside you and walked with you. I have learned so much from my time spent with you all.

To the Phillips Brooks House & Harvard Square Homeless Shelter: thank you for the love, the friendships, all the incredible lessons, and the wonderful memories that I will cherish always.

To my Harvard professors: Thank you for inspiring me to reach even further than I ever thought possible. I'm here now because you pushed me to push myself.

And to everyone else in my life: THANK YOU! I am better for having each of you in this crazy story that is unfolding daily. Here's to the next chapters ... together.

## About The Author

Kody Christiansen's journey from humble beginnings in Fort Worth, Texas, to the distinguished halls of globally renowned universities, is one of extraordinary resilience and determination. Overcoming early life challenges, including his father's imprisonment, the loss of his mother to cancer, and his personal battles with addiction and homelessness, Kody emerged as a symbol of hope and enduring strength.

His award-winning debut memoir, *Hollywood Heartbreak/ New York Dreams,* offers an unflinchingly honest account of his life's struggles and triumphs. His academic successes at NYU, Harvard University, and the University of Cambridge, reflect not only his intellectual rigor, but also his leadership and activism, including his significant work at the Harvard Square Homeless Shelter.

Kody has also made his mark in the entertainment industry, with notable appearances in "Billions," and "A Lover Scorned," and has contributed creatively to both student and independent film projects. Embodying his motto, "Stay Strong and Dream Big," Kody's story is one of relentless resilience and ambition. Kody Christiansen is more than an author; he is a symbol of the belief that no matter the hardships, one can achieve greatness.

Author Bio crafted by Danielle Nuchereno

# Famous Last Words

*Another Ending Becomes the Next Beginning ...*

So, I'll leave you with this. The last words of this anthology will be some of the first words of my next fully fleshed-out memoir. The next book, "The College Years," is already in the works and, boy, are there some stories... NYU, Harvard, Cambridge ... not to mention the summer school adventures (and loves) and, oh, the drama ... so ... much ... drama. But, don't worry, fellow college friend readers, that book is still MANY years away from publication. I have been to quite a few universities ... it may have to be a two-part book!

Thank you all again for going on this journey with me and for sticking with me all these years.
Sending you all the good energy in the world.
As always ... Stay Strong and Dream Big. (Damnit!)
Now, enjoy a sneak peek at Chapter 1 of
"The College Years" .......

## "The College Years"
## Chapter 1: Lights, Camera, and a little Action.

7:00 am on a Tuesday in June. The sun pirouetted its way through my yawning plastic blinders as the air conditioner moved them in rhythm to the sound it hummed. My spacious one-bedroom apartment in the Bronx, the first home I had again after being unhoused for nearly two years in NYC and the place where I was finally able to stick to sobriety, was full of energy on this day. It was a big day — one I had been waiting for my whole life — it was the day I would be flying to Atlanta to film my first co-star role in a film!

The dream didn't come true overnight, of course. This dream was many years in the making, and my sobriety was once again a key that unlocked this opportunity for me. Weeks before I woke up in New York to get ready for a flight, I had been in my other apartment in West Hollywood, preparing for the audition that would lead me to this lifelong goal.

I was working at Hollywood Cakes again part-time and as much as my bicoastal life allowed. I was actually waking up at 8:00 am and getting to the shop by 9:00 to open up and prepare for the day. This version of me was a far cry from the person I used to be when I worked at the cake shop pre-sobriety. Gone were the days of rolling in around 3:00 pm hungover and doing an hour or so worth of work before swiping a few bucks from the petty cash and heading to the gay bars down the street for happy hour. Now, I was the employee that the shop deserved, that my mentor and father figure, Tim, deserved.

It was nice to get to know the customers all over again in this new human form I was in. Some customers I had known for a long time didn't even recognize me — I kid you not, someone asked ME, "What happened to the skinny emo West Hollywood party boy who used to work here?" I thought he was kidding, but he wasn't. Imagine his face when I said, "That was me. I'm that person." Most other clients weren't so oblivious, though, and clearly could remember the mess of a manager I had been when I originally worked there years prior. One in particular saw the changes in me and offered an opportunity that I had been waiting for since that day in my childhood when I first realized I wanted to be an actor; an audition.

Willow Victor of Victorious Casting was one of Hollywood Cake's most loyal and long-term customers. She was also a badass casting director who helped discover some of the biggest actors around today and who worked on many award-winning films and television shows. She told me that she was very proud of the progress I had made and that she was casting a film that would be shot by a two-time Oscar nominee, and would be starring Emilie de Ravin (an actress I had admired since her days on the television show "Once Upon a Time") and would be filmed in Atlanta. She told me the role was that of a gay bartender, and the script had the character in three scenes with multiple lines. She asked me if I could come in the following week to audition for her and the film's producer. I immediately (and gratefully) said yes.

Once I received the page with the lines I needed to learn (called "sides" in the industry) via email, I got to work memorizing and rehearsing. I had to pinch myself a few times while practicing just to make sure I wasn't dreaming. I kept seeing flashes of the barren white walls of the New York homeless shelters in my head even though I was speaking lines into cutely decorated West Hollywood apartment walls. I don't know if I was keeping those scary shelter images close to my mind because I was trying to use it as a visual reminder to remain grateful for how good my life had turned out after beginning my sober journey or was it because I was experiencing PTSD? *That's what it felt like sometimes — the second one.* I wondered how I let myself get so far off track and always felt like if I had just gotten sober sooner — or hadn't started drinking or using drugs at all — I could have been preparing for auditions like this one, many years ago. Coulda, Shoulda, Woulda.

I'm always quite hard on myself. I think most of us are, right? Like, I'd love to meet someone who truly looks in the mirror and doesn't feel like they could change anything or be doing something different with their life. Seriously, if that is you — reach out and tell me your tricks because even when things are calm and I should feel content, that need for *more* creeps up. I think that is human nature. Or maybe it is just *some* humans. But there was no time for regrets or what-ifs — I had to center myself in the present and ace this audition.

So, I practiced. A lot. I ran lines with friends. I recorded myself and replayed it to get things right. And I really visualized myself as the character ... which wasn't too hard, I mean, since I literally *was* a gay (and sober) bartender for a little while at Parigot in NYC before it closed down. I spent the whole weekend preparing, and then on that Monday, I went to work early at the cake shop and counted down the hours to my lunch break and my audition. Tim was very supportive, of course. He ran lines with me in between customers and he was overall very optimistic about this role. He was so proud of me for being 3 years sober at that point and really wanted to see me accomplish my dreams — the ones he always knew I could achieve if I found sobriety. Tim saw it all underneath my addictions, and I'm so grateful he never gave up on me.

11:30 am rolled around, and I was to meet Ms. Victor at 12:15 pm in Westwood. It wasn't too far from the cake shop in West Hollywood, and my BMW Z4 was parked right out front. (Sidenote: another item checked off my vision board was my car. When I was younger, my mom bought me a used silver Mazda Miata - I loved it, and when she died, I bought a new silver Miata, and it always felt like she was with me when I drove it. She was definitely watching over me and the car on the nights my high school bestie, Christy, and I would go car surfing in the fancy neighborhood in Fort Worth called Tara. So, years later, when I first got sober, I put a silver BMW Z4 on that poster board and knew one day I would have it. I bought a beautiful used silver Z4 when I first started my bicoastal life – it was my 2nd-year sober birthday present to myself.) The drive over to Westwood was like slow motion. I knew the lines, I was ready to do it, I think I was just so scared of failure. I had to get this part – not just for me, but for Tim and everyone else who supported me in my life.

I parked in the underground lot and took the elevator up to the 8th floor. The golden bronze glisten of the elevator door reminded me of the elevator at the first homeless shelter in NYC - worlds away from each other, but there was something so similar in that elevating metal box. The start of something new, the anticipation, and the fear — universal feelings, I guess. What was waiting on the other side when the doors opened? My future. My future? Possibilities, for sure. While the shelter was the start of one of the hardest trials of my life, this elevator promised something equally life-changing... or another disappointment.

When the elevator landed, and the bell alerted me that destiny was waiting — I took a deep breath. I immediately heard RuPaul's voice in my head, "And don't fuck it up." I smirked at myself and walked towards the casting office. The lines of the script floated around in my head as I approached the door.

"Hello," I said.
"Hello, Kaleb! Come in, come in."

The welcoming voice was that of the gorgeous and fabulous Willow Victor. Her red hair flowed through the office breeze as she model-walked towards the front desk. She was exactly what you would expect of a high-powered high-class Hollywood casting director. And she was genuinely sweet, kind, supportive, and caring. She told me the producer wanted to see me read for the part and was waiting in the audition room. Wow — that was big. Also, it was super anxiety-producing. But when I walked into the room, it all just faded away.

I ran the lines — did it a couple of times — and when I was finished, she looked at him, he looked at her, and then they both looked at me.

"You're hired," they said in near unison.

I froze momentarily. Flashes ran through my head of me acting out scenes from Buffy and Power Rangers in my front yard with Micheal and James. A literal childhood dream was coming true, and I let out the biggest smile my mouth could stretch. It was like the American Idol judges had just told me, "You're going to Hollywood!" I don't think I had felt this excited about anything in a long time. This would be my second big speaking part (the first one was in Showtime's Billions) and my first time in a film shot in Atlanta.

"Thank you, thank you, thank you," I said, nearly jumping up and down.

"No need to thank us. You earned it," Willow said as she gave me a warm pat on the shoulder. "Now, go get everything lined up. It shoots in a few weeks."

"I will. Thanks again for this opportunity."

And as I left her office door and started down the hallway, she peeked her head outside and said, "Kaleb... great job."

My heart melted. A tear rolled down my cheek. And I gave her another big smile and a nod. I don't think I could even speak for fear that I might start balling with joy. This was a huge moment in my life, and I couldn't wait to tell Tim all about it.

I arrive back at the cake shop about 15 minutes later, parking in front of the shop on Santa Monica Boulevard. I slammed a few quarters into the meter and basically floated into the shop where Tim was at the counter, eyes wide, anticipating some sort of devastating or life-changing news.

"I GOT IT!!"

A big smile came over Tim's face, and he said, "I'm so happy for you, Kaleb. Wow. This is big. Proud of you."

"Thank you! I'm so excited! And I found out that the male lead in the film is going to be Leo Howard."

We quickly googled him, and some pictures of some Disney Channel show popped up, and I was like — umm, what? That can't be him. Then we put "Leo Howard now" into the search bar, and meowww! A handsome, strapping, flexing, young man in his twenties flashes on the screen. "That's my scene partner!!" I yelled. Well, well ... how nice. An opportunity I'd been waiting all my life for AND a good-looking scene partner?! Yes, please.

So, I finished out the rest of the work day at the

shop in a VERY good mood and went back to my apartment to relax and call all of my besties to tell them the amazing news. Lacy was probably the most excited - my twin sister from another mister who is an actress through and through - and of course, Cheri, Jane, Amanda, and Kayla were thrilled, too. I got a lot of "you sure have come a long way" and "so inspired by what you've been able to do since getting sober." And those comments always made me feel good.

It had been three years at that point since I had a sip of booze or a puff or snort of anything. Three years since I barfed on a homeless shelter floor. Three years since I completely hated myself — even though I acted like I loved who I was. Three years since I let the addictions speak for me and then *finally* regained my own power. So, the best comments were always from the people closest to me who had seen me at my worst and were now talking about my progress — my rebirth. I went to sleep that night with a contentment I don't know if I had ever felt before. It was magical.

The next few days were a build-up of excitement, cake shop work, deliveries (*this same time in the summer prior, I was delivering a cake to Beyoncé's baby shower*), and dinner with friends. Jane and I enjoyed some weekly visits to the Rock n' Roll Ralph's on Sunset Boulevard for some deli delicacies and—most importantly—some slices of cake. Even though I worked at a cake shop that made some of the most delicious and extravagant cakes in the world, I always enjoyed a good ol' grocery store cake slice whenever I could get my hands on one. Some sort of comfort food, I guess.

Of course, Jane had also gotten me into yoga around this time which was so perfect in so many ways at the timing of it all. I mean, my first big film role was going to be a gay bartender in a tank top, and I was a few pounds short of my goal weight and definitely was looking for a little more arm definition. So, Jane suggested yoga, and I actually enjoyed it. The teacher was fantastic and played fun pop/rock mixes, so, it was fun—and incredibly sweaty. I also started running at night after work and felt really great about how healthy I was feeling. So, a little cake slice here and there as a "good job" treat was okay.

A week into my new running and healthy-feeling journey, I wrote on my Facebook about how if anyone from my old life, the people who knew the old drunk Kaleb, saw me jogging in exercise clothes, they'd probably be in shock and disbelief. The only time I ever ran during my addiction period was away from drama (that I caused) or towards an open bar. The person I had become in almost three years of sobriety was so far from the meth addict who roamed the streets of West Hollywood looking for some guy for a drug hook-up and a fornicating fling. I felt proud. But I never let the thoughts of who I was before escape my mind. I didn't want to go back to that life — so I had to keep the wound open just a little so I could remember the pain and not make the same mistakes again.

As we got closer to the filming date, I flew back to NYC to check in with my case manager from the Organization that helped me secure and pay for my Bronx apartment (as long as I stayed on track with my sobriety and checked in with them monthly). I had become one of their success stories and one that they would tell new clients about when they came into the Organization to ask for help. That made me proud. Because a lot of people never thought I'd make it out of the darkness that had consumed me for so long. Hell, I honestly didn't think I would either. I still have gold-fish moments where a wave of gratitude washes over me because I still sometimes can't believe the way life turned around for me once I got sober.

Back in my Bronx apartment, the black pleather couch with a Kaleb-shaped indent called my name. I loved that damn couch because it was mine. It was one of the first things I bought after I got that apart-ment and started working again. It held a lot of good memories within its cushions, and, most importantly, it was comfortable. It was "home." I fell into the crev-ice as soon as I dropped my bag on the wooden floor-boards — I was tired from the six-hour flight from Los Angeles, and the anticipation for the week ahead had me a bit nervous. I was going to be in a film, with speaking lines, in a scene with the lead actor — which was my dream.

The nap was well-received (and longer than expected), and I woke up refreshed the next morning and ready to take on the New York City day ahead. I got dressed and headed to the 4 train — I knew I needed to get some steps in and couldn't let all the hard work I had done on my physicality in LA go to waste. Believe me, with the bodega so close to my apartment and their delicious ham and cheese sandwiches with extra mayo or their chop cheeses, I could put back on the pounds I lost in a matter of days. Haha. So, I had to focus. Big dreams - big focus required.

So, I headed down to Union Square to check on my book sales at Barnes and Noble and then planned to head down to Washington Square Park for a little exercise (aka power walking and eye-fucking all the hot men). *((Look, a little mental imaginative sexual and marital fantasies with men I'll never see again didn't hurt anyone. Lol. And, it kept me out of trouble and focused on my goal at hand. I mean, who had time for a real lover?))*

When I disembarked from the 4 train and zigzagged my way through the rambunctious crowd, I made my way up the cement stairs to be welcomed by the familiar sight of Union Square Park and the daily farmer's market glistening in the sunshine. New York

City had its flaws, sure, but there was an indescribable magic that permeated every inch of it. Maybe it was the history, maybe it was energy from the people, or, perhaps, the what-could-be-ness of it all. There was a constant teetering of emotional waves that moved the city — *the ends and the beginnings all wrapped into one.* Glorious and frightening all at the same time.

The Barnes and Noble in Union Square was one of the biggest in the world, one of the most recognizable, and one that I had never thought I would have a book in. But I did. Two books, actually, at this point in time. Both sold well, but it was my first one, Hollywood Heartbreak | New York Dreams, that was always being reordered. The staff there was so nice and so supportive and made sure my book was always on the "Must-Read" table and also prominently placed in the LGBTQ+ sections. This month was June, Gay Pride Month, and the staff told me they ordered a few extra copies and were going to promote it on the "Pride" table at the entrance. Wow! I felt like the luckiest author in the world. Having the support of the staff — especially as a gay independent author — just felt incredible.

So, I signed the copies they had on hand and told them I would be back when the new order came in to sign them, too. My handwritten message in the book? "Stay Strong and Dream Big," of course. My motto. The words I, myself, lived by each day. Stay Strong —

to the commitment I made to myself with sobriety —
and Dream Big — the daily work, small or big, towards
my ultimate goals that spark my heart's desires.

I floated out of the two large and heavy wooden
doors that led out into Union Square and the bustle
of the city. There was something in the air that day -
around 5:25 pm - that caught me by surprise. A little
tingle that said, "Take a turn on East 12th Street today." So, I did.

I walked down University Avenue and then took a
right on East 12th Street — a street I had been on
a couple of times about three years prior during my
momentary sobriety at the second shelter I lived at.
The street which, back then, held a lot of hope for
a homeless and temporarily sober me, was calling my
name yet again. But why? Why now, after the big disappointment I went through the first time? Undoubtedly, it was that whisper of that dream I had dreamed
when I was in high school — going to NYU. On this
street was the admissions office for NYU School of
Professional Studies, which rejected me the first time
I applied, yet here I was again, truly sober and curious
about what could be.

So, I followed the tingle to the front door of the
NYU SPS building and walked in just to see what
might happen. Could one even reapply if they were
rejected? I didn't know. It was the only school I had

applied to during that time — and I wasn't ready back then. I know that. I didn't know that then, but I know it now. I HAD to get rejected from NYU three years prior because I hadn't found my true reason to truly quit alcohol and drugs at that point. I still had two more shelters and a major relapse to experience before I'd find my true sobriety. So, even if I thought I was ready now, could I even reapply? And what would I do about my acting career that was taking off? I mean, I guess it wouldn't hurt to just ask if I could reapply, and then, I could always go back one day if I wanted to. Right?

There was only one way to find out any of it, so I walked in and was greeted by a very warm smile and joyous hello. The security guard, an adorable woman with dark hair and brown eyes, radiated with good vibes and quickly said, "Hello!"

"Hello. My name is Kaleb, and I would like to speak with an admissions counselor if it's possible."

"Oh, honey. It's past 5:00 pm, and I doubt anyone is here, but let me give a quick call upstairs and just check," she says as she picks up the landline phone that sits upon her grey desk.

I think at that point, I was expecting an unanswered call and that awkward silence while we both waited for the 6th and final ring that meant, of course, everyone had left the office by 5:00 pm. But, to my — and the security guard's — surprise, the person on the other end picked up after just one ring.

"Hi, there," the security guard said. "We have a potential student down here who would like to chat with you real quick if you have a second."

The muffled voice said something I was sure was going to be, "I'm already packing up for the day and out the door." But, apparently, it wasn't.

"She said you can go on up. I'll give you access to the elevator."

So, I walked through the electronic gates and stood in front of the elevator as it came down to the ground floor to retrieve me. (Why was I nervous? I don't know. It seemed like elevators were beginning to become a side character in a lot of the interesting moments in my life.) Once the elevator doors opened and I pressed the button, I was on my way.

When the doors opened again on the 3rd floor, I saw the sign that read, "NYU School of Professional Studies - Division of Undergraduate Applied Studies Admissions Office" and made my way around the corner to the front desk. There was no one at the desk, but the admissions associate must have heard the elevator because she popped her head out of her office and said, "Come on in!"

I walked nervously down the tiny hallway, a beautiful view of Manhattan that stretched into the West Village peaked through the blinds on the right, and name placards fastened to doors with degree suffixes and doctoral prefixes to my left. As I arrived 20 feet forward to where her open door was, it hit me; this was really happening. What would I even say? What did I expect to happen?

She motions me into the room and points to the chair in front of her desk. As I sit, she asks for my name and social security number, and then pulls up my file on her computer screen.

"Oh, so, you have applied before, and you were rejected. Hmm... so, why are you applying now? What has changed in the last three years?"

*What has changed in the last three years?*
Everything.


*---- end of chapter draft*

www.ingramcontent.com/pod-product-compliance
Lightning Source LLC
Chambersburg PA
CBHW071353150726

48000CB00001B/8